JOURNEYS

The Journeys series celebrates John Murray's history of publishing exceptional travel writing by rediscovering classic journeys from the past, introduced by today's most exciting writers.

We want the series to capture the wonder that comes from travelling, opening our imaginations to unfamiliar places and cultures, and allowing us to see familiar things through different eyes. These Journeys give fresh perspectives not only on the times and places in which they were originally published, but on the time and place we find ourselves in now.

As a traveller who has walked and written across much of Europe, the author of *Walking the Woods and the Water*, *Where the Wild Winds Are* (both finalists for the Stanford Dolman Travel Book of the Year), and most recently *Outlandish: Walking Europe's Unlikely Landscapes*, I am thrilled to have the role of seeking out these books. Hundreds of suggestions have come to me from the travel writing, nature writing and adventure communities, and also, appropriately enough, through serendipity – one of the titles on last year's list was dropped through my letterbox by a passing neighbour.

In this spirit of chance discovery, we invite your suggestions for books to republish in the future. We are looking for titles currently out of print in the UK, books that have been forgotten about, left to languish on dusty bookshop shelves, or that were unjustly ignored when they were first published – potentially including translated works by foreign language writers. If you have a suggestion, please get in touch with us on Twitter @johnmurrays or @underscrutiny. #JMJourneys

Ni.. H... S..i.s Editor

D1381655

ELLA R. CHRISTIE

THE REMARKABLE STORY OF A WOMAN'S
ADVENTUROUS JOURNEY ALONE THROUGH
THE DESERTS OF CENTRAL ASIA
TO THE HEART OF TURKESTAN

*Through Khiva to
Golden Samarkand*

INTRODUCED BY CAROLINE EDEN

JOHN MURRAY

First published in Great Britain in 2022 by John Murray (Publishers)
An Hachette UK company

1

Copyright © Ella Christie 1925
Introduction © Caroline Eden 2022

A CIP catalogue record for this title is available from the British Library

Paperback ISBN 978-1-399-80570-4
eBook ISBN 978-1-399-80571-1

Typeset in Hewer Text UK Ltd, Edinburgh
Printed and bound in Great Britain by Clays Ltd, Elcograf S.p.A.

John Murray policy is to use papers that are natural, renewable and
recyclable products and made from wood grown in sustainable forests.
The logging and manufacturing processes are expected to conform
to the environmental regulations of the country of origin.

John Murray (Publishers)
Carmelite House
50 Victoria Embankment
London EC4Y 0DZ

www.johnmurraypress.co.uk

Contents

CONTENTS

Introduction

Isabella ('Ella') Robertson Christie (1861–1949) was a shrewd Scottish traveller of rare spirit, born close to my adopted city of Edinburgh. After the death of her father, whom she had cared for until her forties, she set off to explore, fully breaking with ideas of what women should be at that time. Long trips took her into Tibet, Borneo and Kashmir, where she travelled by packhorse and cart to camp in the snow at the Chorbat Pass. But it was her two adventures through Central Asia, in the years leading up to the First World War, in 1910 and 1912, recounted in *Through Khiva to Golden Samarkand* that really stand out. Above all, the great appeal of this book, which has long deserved to be better known, is simple: there is nothing else like it. It stands quietly but magnificently alone.

Ella was the first British woman to visit Khiva, then a remote desert slave-trading town notorious for raiding Turkmen tribesmen, and she was also a member of the Royal Scottish Geographical Society for forty-four years. Tenacious then, yes, but unlike many other travellers of her era she never set out to break records, to spy, to climb mountains or gain accolades. This separates her work from the gung-ho ambitiousness shown by male travelling writers of her generation, such as Arminius Vámbéry, Captain Burnaby, Aurel Stein and Francis Younghusband, many of whom covered similar terrain and were wrapped up in the Great Game, the nine-teenth-century clandestine struggle between the tsarist and British empires. In her introduction, she states her mission: 'My reasons for making the journey were twofold, first, the extreme desire to see for myself what lay on that comparatively bare spot on the map east of the Caspian Sea . . . and secondly, the lure of those magic names, Bokhara and Samarkand'. What we witness, as we follow her from Turkmenistan into Uzbekistan and Kyrgyzstan, is a series of slow-paced expeditions, examining everyday life both high and low, presented in language that is refreshingly inviting, curious and clear-eyed.

What she chose to pack for such journeys, described at the start of the book, hints at where her attention will likely fall along the way, 'a Jaeger rug, and a cotton padded quilt to serve as a mattress, and so help to relieve the unevenness of a Central Asian hotel bedstead . . . a small frying-pan . . . a bag of oatmeal, biscuits, and butter, butter being almost unobtainable throughout Turkestan.' What we quickly ascertain is that Ella cared about, and was captiv-ated by, how people were cooking, what they were bartering for at Silk Road marketplaces and what they were wearing. Topics far more relatable, for most readers, than dusty Great Game politics. She tries the fermented drink kvass, made from rye bread, makes a note of seven different types of raisin at a bazaar, remarks upon how the Turkmen's beloved horses may share their masters' meals and declares Turkmen pears to be far better than 'the finest French ones'. It is kaleidoscopic detail such as this, born of genuine inquisitiveness, that puts you firmly in her leather boots and carries you back in time to faraway cities and desert landscapes. Ella gathered her impressions, whether lounging at a chaikhana or aboard a steamer on the Oxus, by purposefully not rushing through and instead relishing in the joys of simply 'being there'.

Back in Scotland, her home may have been Cowden Castle (thirty miles north-west of Edinburgh and sadly demolished in 1952), but there is a modesty to her, and generally she is more grounded than grand. 'I never had an article stolen or pocket picked. But then perhaps I had nothing worth stealing,' she muses at the end of one chapter. Regularly, she makes charming connections back to her homeland. A sandstorm appears like 'genuine Scotch mist', while cast-off camel wool woven into winter robes reminds her of 'the thrifty days in Scotland long ago, when sheep's wool was carefully collected off hedges and bushes and spun into material'.

During my own journeys through Uzbekistan over the past fifteen years I have often carried Ella's words with me. I remember once escaping a chattering tour group that was dominating a hotel breakfast room in Khiva, to go and sit quietly on a balcony with this book, first published in 1925. As swallows darted over the city's thick eighteenth-century mud walls, I recognized that despite the vigorous restorations that had taken place over many decades, there were still similarities between what I could see and what Ella had described a hundred years earlier: the black elm trees, the swirling dust, figs and vines, ripe melons, tilting minarets, mud walls and single-storey houses with tiny windows. Such scenes are evident, too, in the many photographs Ella took of Khiva – featuring mosques, wells, farmers, carts and caravanserais – with her trusty Kodak camera which, she tells us, often sent local children nervous of the 'evil eye' running. She wasn't the only notable person taking pictures of Uzbekistan's marketplaces and mosques at that time, though. The well-known wandering photographer Sergei Mikhailovich Prokudin-Gorskii was also roving about similar bazaars and deserts between 1910 and 1915, travelling at the command of the last tsar, Nicholas II, who had tasked him with documenting cultures and landscapes of the Russian Empire (1721–1917). Just as Prokudin-Gorskii took photographs of the bread sellers of Samarkand and Turkmen carefully choosing their winter melons in desert landscapes, so did she.

Ella is honest about her concerns, and is not stiff, or squeamish, about recording the hardships and tragedies she witnesses. There is a stomach-curdling passage in Bukhara where she recounts guinea worms being extracted from the legs of the inflicted by barbers ('the surgeons of the community'), and she shows great pity for the blind who often take up the role of masseurs. But especially poignant is her friendship in Khiva with the Russian advisor to the khan, Colonel Korniloff and his wife Natalia Anatolia who are later murdered by the Bolsheviks ('Kind Natalia An., who could then have dreamt of such a fate awaiting you?'). In 1916, after her explorations through Central Asia, Ella oversaw a Red Cross canteen in France, staffed by other Scotswomen, during the Battle of Verdun.

I heard directly about her bravery and doggedness a few years ago, when I was invited to have lunch with her great-nephew, Robert Christie Stewart, at his home in Clackmannanshire. At the dining table, we flicked through boxes of her black-and-white photographs, most no bigger than a playing card, while little trunks were brought out containing souvenirs and ikat textiles that Ella had collected. Robert remembered his great-aunt Ella as a generous woman. But, he added, she loathed social chit-chat. As we ate our soup, Robert explained that once a man on the platform at the nearby railway station in Dollar had casually asked if she was going to Edinburgh for the day. 'No,' Ella shot back. 'I am going to Samarkand!'

Zigzagging and unpredictable, *Through Khiva to Golden Samarkand* is a rare and satisfying book filled with surprise. And it is one that inspires in quite unexpected ways. Just before Ella crossed into Uzbekistan in 1912, travelling by steamer on the Oxus River from Turkmenistan, she made note of a curious carrot preserve. Having never seen such a thing on my own travels, but motivated by her encouraging description, 'a special kind of marmalade made of finely chopped carrots in honey', I recreated a version of it in my kitchen at home in Edinburgh, adding a hint of cinnamon. Not very jammy, but delightful on hot, heavily buttered toast. This edible tribute to Ella has now become a hit and I am rarely without a jar of it.

Caroline Eden, 2022

Through Khiva to
Golden Samarkand

Preface

> Down to Gehenna or up to the throne,
> He travels the fastest who travels alone.

The vast regions of Russian Central Asia are comparatively little known to the outside world, chiefly from the difficulty of persuading those in authority to grant the necessary permission to see any of their Asiatic possessions south of the Siberian Railway. Members of frontier commissions have doubtless crossed it, commercial houses have sent their representatives to the markets of Bokhara, while secret service agents have not been unknown, but the ordinary traveller has seldom been encountered, and since the revolution the isolation has been complete.

My reasons for making the journey were twofold: first, the extreme desire to see for myself what lay on that comparatively bare spot on the map east of the Caspian Sea, a stretch of some 1200 miles to the Chinese frontier; and secondly, the lure of those magic names, Bokhara and Samarkand, renowned in history as well as in the pages of classic tales and poetic fiction for chivalry and romance – a romance which constrained even Milton himself to strike sonorous chords:

> His eye might there command, wherever stood
> City, of old or modern fame, the seat

Of mightiest empire, from the destined walls
Of Cambula, seat of Cathaian Can,
And Samarkand by Oxus, Temir's throne.

The dreary stretches of desert to be traversed might have deterred some, as well as the necessity of having to obtain not only a passport, but also a special permit from the Russian Government. In making application for this, much information had to be supplied: the object of the journey, the exact route to be followed, the stopping-places, and general details, not omitting a certain amount of family history.

These having proved satisfactory, I was told that I might start, though no visible sign or seal was ever put into my hands. The only official paper I had with me was my passport, which had to be given up to the police of the district on arrival at any place in which I intended to pass the night: it could only be reclaimed on the day of departure, and I lived in perpetual dread of having to leave a town without it. All these precautions were in order that the military police might be duly notified, and of course necessitated much time: for my application six weeks were required, and this was considered a record in speed. Whether successful or not, a check is thus supposed to be kept upon the intrusion of undesirable aliens. In my own case, as a woman travelling alone, I almost ranked in that category, as the Russian secret service is so largely recruited from our sex, and officials, wherever met with, never failed to ask: 'Why should you wish to go there? You will have no one to talk to' (an important item in the daily life of a Russian), 'there is nothing to see, travelling is difficult,' and many other such-like trivial suggestions.

Even our own officials did not altogether welcome the idea. I was begged not to get them into any trouble, while the Foreign

Office very kindly warned me in the following letter of the risks I was about to incur were I to persevere in my intention of setting foot in Central Asia. Looking at it in the most favourable light one can hardly say it offered encouragement:

> The sanitary condition of Russian Central Asia and Bokhara is not satisfactory at this moment. There is some plague and much small-pox (both the ordinary and the black variety), scarlet and typhus fevers, and diphtheria. There is also a dearth of vaccine and competent vaccinators.

I pondered over this, not with the idea of its acting as a deterrent, but merely to determine against which of the various diseases mentioned I should take precautions. Finally I decided on small-pox, as it appeared in duplicated form. I was vaccinated in Constantinople, and thought with partial gratitude of Lady Mary Wortley Montagu and her heroic conduct. I suffered tortures for a week, discomfort for much longer, and sympathized with conscientious vaccination objectors. Apropos of this, among the many parting instructions given me was the following: 'Be sure if you take small-pox, at once hang red cloth over the window.' No thought was given as to where red cloth was to be obtained, or if there would be any windows over which to hang it! Having guarded so far against illness, I had to find an interpreter speaking some European language besides Russian. The belief, so current in our country, that all Russians speak French is quickly dispelled in such a search. It is most difficult to get any information on the other side of the Caspian Sea unless one has a knowledge of Russian.

In my two journeys to Central Asia I had experience of two interpreters. One was a Lett who spoke a certain amount of

German, had already knocked about the world in the capacity of a seaman, and who proved to be all that was required. He will be known in these pages under the name of Fritz. The other was a converted Jew, who spoke very 'bookish' English, and who once told me that bishops had sat at his feet, but in what capacity he refrained from divulging. He was far from welcome to officials; indeed, on one occasion, being a Jew, he was forbidden to enter the house of a local governor, and on arrival at Moscow he was ordered to clear out almost as soon as we had arrived. He will be mentioned as the Interpreter.

The question of luggage had next to be thought of; this was necessarily limited as to personal belongings, for I had to take a camp-bed for such occasions when no bedstead was provided, and bed-linen and towels, these not being supplied in hotels, lodgings, or in trains. Sometimes sheets can be obtained by a special arrangement with the landlady, but 'sheets' are usually little better than glorified dusters bordered in red. I had further to provide myself with a Jaeger rug, and a cotton padded quilt to serve as a mattress, and so help to relieve the unevenness of a Central Asian hotel bedstead.

A spirit-lamp with small frying-pan and saucepan proved on many an occasion to be invaluable, and for provisions I had a bag of oatmeal, biscuits, and butter, butter being almost unobtainable throughout Turkestan. The absorbing problem, however, was how to wrestle with the invading hordes of insect life. In an interview that I had with the late Sir Donald Mackenzie Wallace, with reference to travelling in Central Asia, I was warned by him that the ordinary Keating's powder, efficacious in most circumstances, was in these countries of no more use than so much flour, and that a much more powerful destroyer called *Aragatz* must find a top corner in my packing arrangements, as nowhere could one escape from the terror by night!

He also enjoined me, as I valued my life, not to wash even my hands in unboiled water owing to the risk of contracting disease germs. A rubber basin was included, in spite of the further warning of a Russian doctor – 'as to washing the hands, that might be considered, but a wipe of the face with eau-de-Cologne is all I should attempt before returning to the shores of England.' 'The eyes?' 'Yes, a little boric rose water might be thought of.' But, cost what it might, I could not resign myself to this modicum of washing, and realizing the truth of his advice I had to adopt the plan of boiling every drop of water I used all the time I was in Turkestan.

Central Asia may be reached in two ways: either by the Moscow-Orenburg-Tashkent Railway, which takes about five days, or across the Caspian Sea from Baku to Krasnovodsk. In my first journey to Central Asia I chose this latter route, and shall begin the description of my journey on leaving Baku, which is situated on the western side of the Caspian Sea.

The Caspian Sea offers to students of geology many points of interest. At one time, they tell us, it was linked up with the Arctic Ocean by way of the Aral Sea and the River Obi, and in the course of countless ages this vast body of water has gradually diminished till only the Aral Sea and some other desert salt lakes are left. This fact is borne out by innumerable lines and markings along the coast which to the scientist mean the unwritten records of its history. The present level is eighty-four feet below the Black Sea, and is at its highest in the month of July. From the north are poured enormous volumes of water from the two great Russian rivers, the Volga and the Ural, while on the east side practically the only river is the Atrek, which rises in the Kopet Dagh Mountains and skirts the Persian frontier. The immense quantity of fresh water flowing in is diluting by degrees the salt properties; this is especially noticeable in the vicinity of the larger rivers, where the water is salt only to the extent of one per cent., but on the eastern coast it holds a much heavier saline deposit.

The shallower portions are frozen over from November to March, chiefly at the northern end. Navigation then ceases, while in summer on the south end it is also suspended for days at a time from another cause – namely, the violent storms that rage between July and September. The length of the Caspian Sea is 740 miles, and its greatest breadth 300 miles. There is no outlet, and the balance of water is maintained entirely by evaporation.

The salt industry is an important one at various places along the coast, something like 400,000 tons of salt being taken out every year. Krasnovodsk, the chief port on the eastern side, is dependent on the Caspian for its water supply, which is utilized by means of distillation, though some small rain tanks were made by the Russians, and much talk was heard in 1910 of a scheme whereby an improved water supply might be introduced.

Perhaps the most interesting feature of the Caspian is the mysterious current which flows through it, much like the Gulf Stream. It is about 150 feet wide, and runs at the rate of three to five miles an hour. Scientists are not quite agreed as to the cause of this phenomenon. Some maintain that the excess of evaporation on the extensive bay called Karaboghaz, on the east coast, produces an indraught and attracts a larger supply of water to that portion of the sea which rushes through the extremely narrow channel by which the bay is entered. Fishing forms an important industry, especially in the north, where sturgeon, sterlet, and salmon abound, and supply the caviare for which Russia is famed. Seal and porpoises are also inhabitants of the Caspian, and help to bear out the theory that at one time it was joined to the Arctic Ocean.

Anthony Jenkinson on his journey to the Court of Samarkand in the sixteenth century thus reports his knowledge of the Caspian Sea:

This sea is fresh water in many places, and in other places as salt as our great ocean. It hath many goodly rivers falling into it, and it avoideth not itselfe except it bee underground. During the time of our navigation wee sett up the redd crosse of S. George in our flagges, for honour of the Christians, which I suppose was never seen in the Caspian Sea before.

At Baku I was warned that it was dangerous to eat fish caught near there, even salmon having been known to produce blood poisoning, although no reason could be given for the cause of such unpleasant consequences.

Having been seen safely on board by the police at Baku, I watched the shores of Europe disappear in a cloud of lights as we sailed off about eight P.M. The steamer was crowded with Asiatic natives of all kinds, who sprawled all over the deck and found accommodation for the night amid bundles of a most miscellaneous description, my introduction to the travelling impedimenta of that part of the East. The cabin was quite comfortable though the berth was unfurnished, and having unpacked and spread out my quilt and sheets, I made the best of a somewhat 'roll-y' passage till, after a twelve hours' voyage, calm was reached in the harbour of Krasnovodsk next morning. There I was again met by the police, a somewhat novel attention, and one to which I was hitherto unaccustomed. The necessary formalities of examining my passport had to be gone through, objections raised in hope of a stray rouble, much talk to be listened to and interpreted, until finally I was allowed ashore to enjoy my first sight of Central Asia.

I

My First Sight of Central Asia

My first sight of Central Asia is a memory of temporary-looking houses and clouds of sandy dust, known under the name of Krasnovodsk. The situation of the town somewhat resembles Aden, with its bare brown rocks and the same guarding line of rocky islands in the mouth of the harbour. On its quays may be seen mountainous bales of raw cotton ready for shipment to the mills of Moscow and other manufacturing towns in Russia, while European goods of all kinds supply the requirements and gratify the tastes of ten to twelve million inhabitants of Central Asia, who, year by year, are discarding their native-made articles in favour of Western goods, which in many cases is to be deplored.

As regards dwellings, nothing of a more permanent nature is to be seen than the station buildings, substantially built of stone, where I managed to obtain quite a good meal of roast meat and stewed dried apricots before starting on the journey to Ashkabad at four P.M. The officials in charge of the station have the air of men undergoing a term of banishment, anxious to learn 'how soon can we be out of this?' The answer to this query for the traveller means some hours, as there is only one train each way in the twelve hours. The railway was constructed in 1880 by General Skobelof, the conqueror of Turkestan, as a military one, and as a military one it is still maintained. Originally it was intended to go only as far as Ashkabad, but the rapid development of cotton-growing led to its extension eastwards to the more fertile province of Ferghana, and the terminus is now reached at Andigan, a distance of nearly a thousand miles from Krasnovodsk, and about ninety from the frontier of Chinese Turkestan. The war of 1881 secured this stretch of country for Russia, and at Geok Teppe was fought the last battle with the Tekke Turcomans, the native inhabitants of that part of the country west of the Oxus. Thousands of them were slaughtered, and their fort, formerly a Persian one, was razed to the ground. Fragments of the surrounding mud wall testify to its size, and to its inadequacy to cope with modern implements of war. As a testimony to the administrative qualities of the conquerors, squadrons of native cavalry, officered by them, may be seen exercising in the vicinity, an arrangement which still allows scope for the fighting instincts of a fine people.

The railway line is suitable for a certain amount of heavy traffic, and the engines are powerful ones, built chiefly in Moscow. They are in most cases petrol-driven, and in order to maintain the supply, pipes of oil are laid on from wells along the railway track to reservoirs at certain stations; in some cases it is even carried in boiler-like receptacles on wagons.

The line is not ballasted, but simply levelled up, and the rails are spiked on to the sleepers, which last are chiefly made of pine-wood from the Volga district. Wood for that purpose is unobtainable nearer at hand, and even for fuel for stoking the engines, where petrol is not employed, the roots and branches of an insignificant-looking shrub called *saxaul* is the only kind available throughout Turkestan.

The trains are usually made up of first, second, third and fourth class carriages; these last are practically no better than horse-boxes. The railway gauge is eight inches wider than that of Europe, which allows of wider carriages, and they are consequently built higher in proportion.

The first and second class, which are corridor carriages, are not uncomfortable; the seats, covered in red-and-white-striped cotton material, form beds during the night, and there is a curb chain which secures the door firmly inside. By a small payment the compartment can be reserved. Heating is arranged for by a stove at the end of the carriage, which keeps it suffocatingly hot; added to which – as the windows of the carriages are often double – it is almost impossible to obtain fresh air. There is economy of light both by day and night, for the windows are small, high up, and on one side of the carriage only, that on the corridor side being entirely panelled in wood, so that it is difficult to see the scenery except when it is occasionally reflected by a mirror in the door. Above the door is a tin lamp in which is a candle, the only means of dispelling the darkness when night falls.

This is typical of Russian methods, for sometimes elaborately built stations have nothing more than a tin lantern to light them, as if the energy that started building them had given out. 'Russia is so prone to lose heart, to fluctuate in her desires, and grow weary of her dreams,' and the same falling off from big beginnings applied to requests for information and plans. For example, in referring to officials I would state what was required, and in the most courteous manner would be told nothing could be easier than to carry out my wishes, but when it came to details all the fine ideas vanished like mist. Again and again this happened, and I cannot but feel that something – I do not know whether to call it practicality or perseverance – is greatly lacking in the Russian character.

My experience in reference to this point coincides with that of Monsieur Paléologue, who in his *Memoirs* recently published thus describes this aspect of the Russian character as he found it:

> I put him [M. Dormer] on his guard against the facility with which Russians seem to acquiesce straight off in every-thing proposed to them. It is not duplicity on their part. Far from it! But their first impressions are usually inspired by their feelings of sympathy, a desire to please, the fact that they hardly ever have a strong sense of reality, and the receptitude of their minds which make them extremely impressionable.

The trains are run by Petrograd time, so each station clock has two pointers, one painted black to indicate rail time, while local time is shown by the pointer painted red. Three men are employed to check the tickets and, I suppose, each other's dishonesty. At every stopping-place a table is set out on the platform on which are steaming samovars (the well-known Russian brass tea urn), and piles of excellent white bread, eggs and bottles of milk. Superior tables can sometimes offer *blinskys*, which are thin pancakes enclosing minced meat. These when hot are not unpal-atable, but when half cold the mutton fat, in which they are cooked, makes itself too pronounced. Tumblers of pale-coloured tea are welcomed on these long dusty journeys, especially by the native travellers, to allay the thirst produced by the constant eating of sunflower seeds. This is almost the equivalent of the chewing-gum of America, being more used as a means of passing the time than as an actual food. I tasted the seeds and found them uninteresting. Their husks bestrew the floor of every carriage (laid with linoleum or wax-cloth), and every few hours an official goes round with a hard whisk to clear away all debris. The more important stations have buffets, which also serve as waiting-rooms, and the station is used as a meeting-place of the whole district on the arrival and departure of trains, the chief event in the twenty-four hours in these remote regions. This description applies to the arrangements regarding trains and travelling before the revolution.

The Russians are said to pride themselves on mixing with the natives, a laudable idea if only a little more space at the stations were given to do so. My thoughts conjure up a crowded junction when all and sundry were packed into the one room, and particularly a lively experience at Tchernaivo, the hour two-thirty A.M., the room filled with piles of bundles – luggage in Central Asia does not run to boxes, and only to an occasional carpet bag or suit-case – tired Russian mothers with an air of resignation equally shared by their children, even including the inevitable infant, trying to find a corner for repose among their belongings. Each girl's head is tied up in a handkerchief, the counterpart of her mother's, but boys are in strange loofah helmets. The group is composed of various nationalities, some drinking tea and some trying to sleep, while in the corner is ranged the never-failing bookstall for the sale of post-cards, chiefly those of an objectionable kind. At the fly-covered bar, adorned with bottles and *blinskys*, are groups of men indulging in vodka and endless talk. Struggling through the semi-darkness to find one's train, one stumbles across strange white-sheeted figures, their faces turned towards Mecca, kneeling on some vestige of a sacred rug, faithful to the forms of their religion as first inculcated by Mahomet on Arab plains so far removed by space and centuries.

II

The Journey Across the Desert to Ashkabad

*Patient Travellers – Dunes and Deserts – Russian
Forestry – Irrigation Work – George IV. Guns –
Khalats – Native Bazaars – Promiscuous 'Smokes'*

One Moment in Annihilation's Waste,
One Moment, of the Well of Life to taste –
The Stars are setting and the Caravan
Starts for the Dawn of Nothing – Oh, make haste!

After unrolling one's bundles and settling oneself as comfortably
as circumstances permitted in the somewhat restricted space of a
Central Asian railway carriage, on the ringing of the last of the
three warning bells, the train glided out of Krasnovodsk at eight
P.M. At stopping-places by the way these bells were a constant
source of anxiety, it was so easy to miss one. Ashkabad was reached
next day at midday; not a very rapid transit considering the
distance, which is 220 miles; but I found on long journeys this
slower mode of progression to be much less tiring than are our
express trains, and besides I do not suppose the line as laid would
stand their vibration.

The stations along the route are well built of stone, the platforms paved with brick, set edge up in herringbone pattern, and

crowds are always assembled at them, as the Russians encourage railway travel among the natives, while they in turn think nothing of waiting for hours, or even days if need be, and happily camp on the platform during the enforced delay. Their name for the railway train is 'Sheitan Arba,' or the devil's coach!

For a considerable distance after leaving Krasnovodsk the journey presents few features of interest, as about two-thirds of the country of Turkestan is desert through which oases are scattered. It is bounded on the south by a continuous chain of mountains which contribute the water supply of the five rivers by which the country is intersected. Of these rivers the Amu Daria or Oxus and the Syr Daria or Jaxartes, both falling into the Aral Sea, are the most important, while the other three, the Mourghab, the Tedjen and the Zerafshan, are lost in marshes or form small lakes. The desert between the Caspian Sea and Amu Daria is known as the Kara-Kum, but one must not imagine it as all a flat plain, for in parts it rather resembles a troubled sea of sand, whose dunes reach as high as sixty feet, their crescent-shaped surface rippled as by a tidal wave. These dunes are of so shifting a nature as to endanger the lives of any who seek to find a track across these desolate wastes. An interesting allusion to these sand-holes is to be found in an account of his journey by an ambassador to the Court of Tamerlane, in which he states that on the banks there were great plains of sand, and the sand was moved from one spot to the other by wind, and was thrown up in curious semicircular mounds, and the wind blew the sand from one mound to another, for it was very light, and on the ground where the wind had blown away the sand the marks of the mounds were left.

In another description a Roman historian Quintus Curtius (translated in 1553) notes: 'To observe the starres as they do, that sayle the seas, and by the course of them direct their journey, wherefore in the daye time the country is wild and impassable, when they can finde no track nor waye to go in, nor marke or sign whereby to passe.'

These descriptions apply absolutely to the present-day condition of that treeless waste, as well as to the time in which they were written. At intervals, instead of sand-dunes there are flatter stretches, whitened by saline deposits, with but scanty signs of vegetation, and yet amid this apparent desolation one knows that wherever irrigation is introduced a Garden of Eden is sure to follow.

In parts the railway has to be protected from sand-blocks by thick fences of thorn and scrub planted at each side, which somewhat check the inroads made by sandstorms, especially at that part known as 'the caravans' graveyard,' a name that tells its own tale.

The Russians in laying out their new towns have made the invariable rule of building them entirely apart from the native ones; it might be two or it might be ten miles off, according to circumstances. This has enabled them to build unhampered by space, and regardless of the extent of ground required for their laying out. Wide avenues of trees in double and even treble rows, with rivulets trickling between the rows, are much to be commended, the general plan being not unlike that of our Indian cantonments, while the railway station at Ashkabad was, like most of those already passed, a well-built stone one, with quite a pretentious façade on the town side.

Ashkabad boasts of avenues of poplars and acacias, with one-storey bungalows buried in greenery, and rather feeble attempts at gardens. Nasturtiums, stocks, and most of our garden flowers would grow if encouraged, but the average Russian officer's wife either has other things of more real importance to occupy her, or lacks a pride in making her home look attractive.

In the town are various public buildings, such as schools and technical colleges, and in the principal square there is a Russian church, with its fine gilded domes; in front of it in this square are some old brass guns, with the royal monogram of our King George IV. – a strange place to meet them, and evidently they must at some period have been taken from the Afghans, to whom we had given artillery.

There was also at the time of my visit a large temple in process of erection by the sect of the Bahais, which has many adherents among the Persians. There is a considerable trade with Persia, as the frontier is only a few miles distant, and Meshed, 180 miles to the south, draws many Mahometan pilgrims to its shrine.

The chief attraction of the native quarter is its market, for there may be seen the many varieties of inhabitants of the country; prominent among them are of course the Tekke Turcomans, a fine-looking race in their dark-red-striped *khalats*, as their long robes are called, very similar in shape to a dressing-gown, a gaily coloured sash-band tied round their waists, on the head a huge fur cap of either black or white astrakhan, and high soft leather boots. The market is a very extensive one, held on a large open place, where the more luxurious merchants erect sheds or tents for them-selves. One side of the square is devoted to quadrupeds, of which the camels form the noisiest and most noisome section. They are of the Bactrian breed, larger and heavier than those of Arabia, and in winter are covered with immensely thick brown wool, which as the warmer weather approaches is shed in handfuls, leaving large unsightly-looking bare patches. Their cast coats are not, in another sense, thrown away, for the wool is carefully collected and skilfully woven into the long robes of their owners, or else it is used for stuffing quilts, which are the native substitutes for blankets, deliciously warm and light. This reminds one of the thrifty days in Scotland long ago, when sheep's wool was carefully collected off hedges and bushes and spun into material for household use.

In another part of the market is to be seen cotton in its raw state, as well as cotton seed, both whole and crushed, testifying to a growing industry, of which the climax is reached in Ferghana, the most easterly province of Russian Central Asia. A rather uncommon use is made of the cotton seed, besides the ordinary one of oil-cake. The seed is crushed and then moulded into the form of a jug with a short spout, in which is contained the oil which has been already expressed from the small brown seeds.

Earthenware dishes for household use are displayed by another dealer – the inside of the flat dishes are coloured blue or green, with a fine glaze – while a collection of unglazed water-jars, whose artistic forms are strongly reminiscent of the Greek occupation, stand on the ground. A pile of rather squat ones, with a knob at the bottom, are intended for use on irrigation wheels, and this projection enables them to be securely tied on.

In a corner in a shed is found a copper mender, where fluted copper and brass jugs, or perhaps more strictly ewers, known as *kungana* by the natives, in every stage of dilapidation have been entrusted to his repairing powers. With the simplest of tools and means at his command, he appears to be able to make every dent vanish; a hammer and crooked stick seem to do the trick, while leakages are stopped with equal success. The copper vessels, sometimes plated with zinc and ornamented with tracery, are not unlike Kashmir work, the true Central Asian specimens depending solely on form and fluting for decoration. By way of additional adornment, jugs or ewers are sometimes chased by modern workers to imitate Indian work, which quite spoils the original design. So attractive are the purely fluted ewers that one hopes it may be long before the enamelled iron introduced by the Russians takes possession of the homes of such an artistic race.

In another corner of the mender's shed I was suddenly confronted with a sight that for a moment filled me with horror. Tales of decapitation in public places flashed into my mind as I seemed to see a place of execution. Rows of astrakhan heads on poles turned out after all to be nothing more alarming than a hat stall. It shows what imagination can do, when I pictured a head inside each one of them.

The fruit stalls of the market offer immense choice in raisins; on one stall alone I counted seven varieties. Their uses are many: they are sold mixed with parched peas, which the natives crunch in handfuls; they are also cooked in the national dish of *pilau*, and further are employed in making raisin wine, a somewhat sweet syrup. A fruit new to me was the *puchara*, rather like an undersized Tunis date, with a reddish yellow papery skin, the inside being of a floury consistency and a pleasant acid flavour. The melon stall has many customers: one cannot think of any market in Turkestan without associating it with large rose-pink slices whose black seeds give an accentuating note of colour. By means of some secret of preserving them they can be had in a fresh state all the year round. The process is said to consist of burying them in the sand, and doubtless the extreme dryness of the atmosphere assists to bring about the result.

Seeing several stalls furnished with sacks of what at first I took to be fragments of dark coloured cement bricks, I asked what species of building material they represented, and was told they were the refuse of black bread discarded by the soldiers months previously, and sold in this state to make *kvass*, a favourite Russian drink somewhat resembling very light beer, but such previous treatment did not make one specially anxious to sample it when occasion offered.

Strolling among the crowd is a prominent object, the itinerant smoke vender, offering a smoke of his *chilim* or native pipe for the fraction of a farthing, but how many draws are allowed I never ascertained. The pipe itself is a gourd of artificial shape, mounted in brass. On the top is fixed a terra-cotta receptacle to hold the ashes and tobacco, or else it may be *mahorka*, a preparation of hemp seed, somewhat narcotic in its effect. At the side is inserted a bamboo stem, and it is the business of the vender to see that it is in proper working order, and if the smoke be not to his satisfaction a customer may return the pipe and ask him to make it draw. This indiscriminate use of the same mouthpiece seems to offer no objections, and these can hardly be raised when the price of a smoke is less than a quarter of a farthing.

After all this was no worse than what was the practice in my youth of the general 'merchant' of a certain country village. Being of an obliging nature, when it came to selling tooth-brushes, he used to beg his customers: 'Tak' hame twa three o' them an' see which ye like, an gie me back the rest'!

Or again, I remember seeing in America a pawnshop in whose window was a small tray laid out with plates of false teeth with this tempting invitation on a large label: 'Try us'!

Amid all the throng there are few foot-passengers. Like the southern Irish, no self-respecting native would dream of being seen otherwise than on the back of a quadruped, even if only a donkey, and two and even three may be seen riding an animal at the same time. How the third manages to cling on to some diminutive pony's back was at all times a problem to me. One of the most remarkable features in a native crowd is the almost total absence of women. A figure swathed in a long cloak and peeping through a horsehair face-covering may be noticed at rare intervals, but for the most part the women are never seen unless in the tents of nomadic tribes.

Ashkabad has the advantage of a river near by, the Mourghab, which the interpreter informed me was one of the four that flowed out of the Garden of Eden!

III

Raids & Raiders

/

> And fairest of all streams the Murga roves,
> Among Merou's bright palaces and groves.

Thus sang Tom Moore of the Garden of Eden river, but I fear if he had seen the reality his song would have been less tuneful. Merv, or known by the more musical form of Merou in Persian, once the 'Queen of the World,' is now a vast plain of shapeless mounds, an occasional remnant of a building rising out of the debris. Its modern counterpart is called Bairam Ali, and New Merv is a separate town seventeen miles distant, 487 miles south of the Caspian Sea. The situation of Old Merv on the Mourghab river offered the most ample facilities for commerce, while its system of irrigation from the same source was taken full advantage of from very early times and reckoned one of the wonders of the world. Its foundation is lost in the mists of antiquity, but it already ranked as an important town when the province was under the sway of the Parthians.

Then a dazzling procession of conquerors tramped through its borders, Darius the Persian, Alexander the Great, the Roman

Emperors, the Caliphs of Mahomet, Ginghiz Khan, Tamerlane, and finally the overwhelming hosts of Russia, from first to last all telling the same tale of slaughter and spoliation, destruction and death. In the fifth century a less belligerent spirit was abroad, and before the sixth century was reached Merv and Samarkand were both the sees of bishops of the Nestorian Church. Within a few years of the death of Mahomet his followers had overrun Persia preparatory to seizing on the town of Merv. 'The Caliph Othman promised the government of Khorasan to the first general who should enter that large and populous country, the kingdom of the ancient Bactrians. The condition was accepted, the prize was won; the standard of Mahomet was planted on the walls of Herat, Merou, and Balkh; and the successful leader neither halted nor reposed till his foaming cavalry had tasted the waters of the Oxus.'

In 705 Kutayba, the camel-driver, made a triumphal entry into Merv as governor of Khorasan, and the city then served as the headquarters from which he carried hostilities into the neighbouring provinces. We are not told if the merciful instructions as issued by Abu Beker, father-in-law of Mahomet, were followed on those expeditions, but they cast a ray of humanity down the ages and serve to lighten a dark page of history. 'Remember,' said the successor of the Prophet, 'that you are always in the presence of God, on the verge of death, in the assurance of judgment, and in the hope of Paradise avoid injustice and oppression; consult with your brethren, and study to preserve the love and confidence of your troops. When you fight the battles of the Lord, acquit yourselves like men, without turning your backs; but let not your victory be stained with the blood of women or children. Destroy no palm-trees, nor burn any fields of corn. Cut down no fruit trees, nor do any mischief to cattle, only such as you kill to eat. When you make any covenant or article, stand to it, and be as good as your word.' Do not these instructions show the decadence of civilization, when one pictures the onslaught of the Germans on the innocent inhabitants of Belgium and the endless laying waste of the orchards and vineyards of France?

The spirit of the Prophet's words pervaded the conduct of Alp Arslan, the 'valiant lion,' as his name implies, the victorious conqueror of the Roman Empire in Asia in 1072. His equanimity and generosity to his foes show the highest type of valour, and indeed were the indirect cause of his death. After a triumphant march from Bagdad, during which he crossed the Oxus with an army of 200,000 men, taking twenty days in the passage, he was about to deal leniently with the captive general at his feet, who instead of appreciating such generosity drew a dagger and mortally wounded him. His dying words were a humble testimony to his character. 'In my youth,' said Alp Arslan, 'I was advised by a sage to humble myself before God; to distrust my own strength; and never to despise the most contemptible foe. I have neglected these lessons; every neglect has been deservedly punished. Yesterday, as from an eminence I beheld the numbers, the discipline and the spirit of my armies, the earth seemed to tremble under my feet; and I said in my heart, Surely thou art the king of the world, the greatest and most invincible of warriors. These armies are no longer mine; and, in the confidence of my personal strength, I now fall by the hand of an assassin.' The remains of the Sultan were deposited in the tomb of the Seljukian dynasty, and the passenger might read and meditate this inscription: ' "O ye who have seen the glory of Alp Arslan exalted to the heavens, repair to Meru, and you will behold it buried in the dust." The annihilation of the inscription, and the tomb itself, more forcibly proclaims the unstability of human greatness' (Gibbon).

This golden period of material prosperity, literature, and the fine arts extended until the rising of nomadic tribes brought grief to the heart of Sultan Sanjar, the grandson of Alp Arslan, through the treachery of Atziz, 'Grand Ewer-Bearer' to the Sultan. The nomadic tribes of the Khanates of Khiva rose in revolt and, after various reverses, finally defeated Sultan Sanjar and his army of 100,000 men. This opened the way to the capital, Merv, and left that opulent city as the prey of the invaders. 'The greedy nomads, spurred to madness by the sight of so much wealth, seized all that met their eyes, and then tortured the inhabitants till they revealed their hidden treasures.'

Sanjar remained four years a captive, during which time his wife acted as queen regent. After her death in 1156, seizing a favourable moment to escape, he reached his capital, only to die of a broken heart at the desolation that met his eyes. He was revered as a second Alexander the Great, and earned the love of his subjects to such a degree that they prayed for him for long after his decease. He was a special patron of Persian poetry. His tomb at Merv, built by himself, is now one of the most important ruins, and so enduring was it believed to be that he called it the Abode of Eternity. Sixty years after his death it was destroyed by Ginghiz Khan, and earthquakes have not spared it, but the memory of the Sultan saint still lives in the hearts of the people, as testified by the numerous offerings still laid upon his shrine.

The next overwhelming disaster that overtook Merv was the incursion of the Mongol hordes led by Ginghiz Khan. Of insignificant origin, born of the tribe of black Tatars in the region of Mongolia in 1162, this remarkable man rapidly rose to fame. When little more than a youth he assembled a diet of the nobles, constituted himself their leader, and assumed the title of Ginghiz Khan, which means 'the very mighty king.' He captured Merv and, it is said, put over a million of the inhabitants to death. This may possibly be an exaggeration, though the Mongol method of numbering the slain should have made for accuracy – every thousandth corpse was buried head downwards, with the feet sticking up. He burned and looted to such an extent that it was long before the city even partially recovered in the one hundred and fifty years of Mongol rule.

A similar scene reopens with the ravages of Timur or Tamerlane. A scion of a noble family in the village of Shakr-i-sabz, forty miles south of Samarkand, in the year 1336, at the age of twelve, he was already dreaming of conquests, and at the age of twenty-five was regarded as the saviour of his country. Success followed his arms, but nothing short of the conquest of the world could appease such ambitions as possessed him, not even the twenty-seven crowns which he had himself placed upon his head. It is said that 'the power of his civil as well as military government consisted in a deep knowledge of other countries, which he acquired by his interviews with travellers and dervishes, so that he was fully acquainted with all the plans, manoeuvres, and political movements of foreign courts and armies.' 'His successors reigned but they did not govern,' and consequently the Central Asia possessions fell into the hands of the Uzbegs, and subsequently into those of the Persians.

In the fifteenth century Merv was rebuilt, and its possession alternated between those two peoples until 1795, when the Emir of Bokhara killed the Persian governor of Merv, and once more the Uzbegs were in the ascendant. They utterly demolished the town, and destroyed the dam at Sultan Beim which helped to fill the canals and streams, hoping thereby to turn the fertile lands into a desert, as a defence against the Persians, as well as deporting 40,000 of the inhabitants to Bokhara. Later the Bokhariots used it for what could now be called a convict settlement. Local raids disturbed the country at intervals until the final annexation by Russia in 1881.

The ruins cover a space of about thirty square miles, surrounded by remnants of the walls, and a towered gateway gives access to a large square with fragments of buildings, the remains of the fortress destroyed by the Emir of Bokhara. A still larger space is known as Abdullah Khan Kalah. The Nestorians lived in the part known as Giaour Kalat. Little has been done in the matter of excavation, and it is questionable whether such would repay the time and trouble of such a work. The houses, being probably built of sun-dried bricks, would contain no durable qualities, and when one thinks of the thoroughness with which towns were sacked and burned by these far-off conquerors the chances are exceedingly small that anything of interest would be left.

> The pestilence, the desert spear
> Smote them; they passed with none to tell
> The names of them that laboured here;
> Stark walls and crumbling crucible,
> Strait gates, and graves, and ruined well,
> Abide, dumb monuments of old,
> We know but that men fought and fell,
> Like us – like us – for love of gold.
>
> ANDREW LANG

IV

The Oasis of Merv

*Agricultural Encouragement – Tekke Turcoman
– Huts – The Tsar's Farm – A Day in the
Country – High Life – Modern Merv*

Leaving the desolation of Old Merv, we come to the oasis of Merv, which has about 16,000 square miles under cultivation, but outlines of canals show to what a much larger extent the land was developed in former days. The chief crops raised are wheat, rice, cotton, barley, sesame (an oil-producing seed), and sorghum, which is a species of millet; while the fruits are famed: grapes, peaches, apricots, and melons, these last naturally forming a large proportion of the food of the population.

In the matter of forestry the Russian Government has done much for the country, planting vast quantities of poplars and willows that find their natural soil by the water-courses, and mulberries, whose leaves are employed to feed the silkworms, in order to develop still further the silk trade. Large quantities of the raw silk are exported to France, and when I asked the reason why factories were not established in Turkestan, to thus save the freight, I was told it cost less in the end, as labour was so much cheaper in France, and women could be employed there in the factories.

The Tekke Turcomans, who are the dominating race in Turkestan, have vast herds of camels, horses, cattle, sheep, and goats. The horses are wonderfully strong, well-bred little animals, and their endurance on long journeys is proverbial, travelling sixty to seventy miles a day for several days on end, fortified, it is often said, by the balls of barley meal and sheep's-tail fat given them on such occasions. As a rule their feeding consists of barley and chopped straw, but, if necessary, they have even been known to share their master's meal of *pilau*. They are never stabled, but merely picketed in the open, covered with layers of felt clothing, the number of rugs increasing according to the age of the horse.

The Tekke Turcomans live in huts of tent shape, *kibitka* as they are called. The process of their erection is very simple. A framework is first made of poplar poles; this is covered with felt and reed mats, while inside the huts are lined with carpets, in the making of which the Turcomans are famed, though Russian taste and aniline dyes are fast destroying the native colouring. The food of the people consists chiefly of mutton, fruit, and vegetables; butter is unknown, but milk of various animals in the form of a kind of Devonshire cream, or cream cheese, is much used. Their women are not 'purdah,' and are even unveiled, though a coquettish jewelled fringe surrounds their foreheads, partially concealing their eyes.

The women's robes in shape much resemble those of the men, and are made of sheep or camel wool. The men invariably wear the *khalat* and sheepskin head-coverings, and full trousers tucked into long boots, with the strange appendage of high heels – patches of shagreen are added for smart effect. The mountain boots have turned-up toes and high pointed heels, to which are added spikes to give additional foothold on precipitous paths, and must be most uncomfortable wear. Worn with those boots are

chamois-leather trousers, of ample volume, elaborately embroidered in red and green silk – the work of the women.

After the annexation by Russia the first thing done was to try
to improve the irrigation works in order to increase the wealth of
the country, and for this purpose the services of the late Sir Colin
Scott-Moncrieff were placed at the disposal of the Russian
Government, with gratifying results, for something like 200,000
acres were thereby gained and handed over to the Tsar Alexander
II. in order that experiments of all kinds might be tried in agriculture and fruit-growing. This tract of land is near Old Merv, or
Bairam Ali, as it is now called, and the Tsar settled some three
hundred emancipated serfs to help to colonize it. Fruit trees of all
kinds were planted; the results exceeded the highest anticipation,
the pears even surpassing the finest French ones. Vines were grown
in order that their produce might supply the great demand for
raisins, and also as a means of helping the wine trade, while other
fruits were canned and made into preserves. I spent a most interesting day among ancient ruins and modern cultivation. Having
wired to the manager of the estate, who lived at the Tsar's residence, much to the perturbation of the interpreter, who tried to
emphasize his social standing by explaining: 'But you see he is a
great man' (the manager). 'Never mind,' I said, 'put it as politely
as you can, and say I was told by the Petrograd authorities to
address myself to the officials.' But receiving no reply from them,
owing no doubt to Russian dilatory habits, I went on my way.

For those desiring to visit Old Merv, or Bairam Ali – so named
after a Persian chief who protected the people of Merv from
marauding bands in the eighteenth century – it is necessary to stay
at the Russian town of New Merv, about seventeen miles distant,
in order to find accommodation. In about an hour by train we
reached our objective, and at the station a smart *troika* was

waiting, in response to my appeal. Three fine horses formed the team; the two outer ones galloped along, their necks curved outwards, while the middle one trotted for all he was worth in order to keep pace with the other two. The coachman was of portly build, in a scarlet shirt, while on his head he wore a low-crowned white beaver hat with a mother-of-pearl buckle in front.

Inside the *troika* was seated a female, her head rolled in a white scarf, who hailed me in English. She proved to be the *gouvernante*, or lady housekeeper, sent to meet me. We drove to the palace, where I was received by the manager, General Alexander Mikhailov, who apologized for the absence of his wife, who was spending the day in Merv.

A handsome stone residence had been built for the manager, or possibly it was erected on such a scale on the off chance of a visit from the Tsar himself, and it was even provided with marble baths, which were proudly displayed to me.

How little could any of us have then guessed that within five years British troops would find accommodation beneath its roof. The rooms were large and lofty; an icon, with its little red lamp burning in front of it, hung in the corner of each one, but otherwise there was no attempt at furnishing as we know it in our homes.

I was given *déjeuner* while the General sat by playing patience and chewing dried apricots, which seemed rather odd behaviour at lunch. At the conclusion of the repast a samovar was brought in and tea was served, accompanied by an excellent liqueur neither strong nor sweet, after which the *troika* was again ordered to take me round Old Merv.

Mrs Snowden, the lady housekeeper, was my escort, and talked all the time, pouring out the entire family history like the pages of a Russian novel, which enabled me to glean who everyone was and the history of those carrying on this work, while we galloped along on our way to Old Merv. She herself was half Italian and half German, and was married to an Englishman, which qualified her on his death for coming to Russia as an English governess. She remained on in the General's household as *gouvernante*, and had a board hung on the wall of her room on which were suspended all the palace keys – rather a confiding way of guarding them.

We careered wildly over fallen grandeurs, the outside horses leaping over every obstacle, and every bell jingling on the gaily decorated harness. The coachman apparently had every reliance on himself, driving with a rein in each hand as is the Russian custom. I remarked to Mrs Snowden, in order to gain, if possible, something of confidence, that he seemed a careful driver, when my fears were far from being allayed by her saying: 'Yes, he has been seventeen years with us, but he still has accidents; last week he stuck in a hole and upset the carriage!' Of course if one could have seen the track, the mounds, the crevasses we cleared, such a statement would have caused no surprise. Through it all the old lady sat unmoved, but surreptitiously I had to grasp the low side of the *troika*.

At length we arrived without accident at the orchards, which were over a thousand acres in extent, and were impressed with all the Russians had done. Everywhere wells were being bored – one had to be sunk 700 feet deep before reaching water – and an American company were devising pumps by which to get the water raised.

After our perilous drive we returned to the palace, where hospitality was again offered in the shape of tea, and then I was pressed to join in a game of tennis with the house party and a few of their friends.

Without disgracing myself I might have taken part, for what kind of play can be expected of officers in full uniform and military caps on their heads? For I found that it was considered quite impermissible for an officer to appear without his coat in the company of ladies.

The following day as I passed through Bairam Ali the General's wife and Mrs Snowden came to the train to see me, bearing an offering of a bunch of mauve irises and lilac stuck in a mushroom-pickle bottle with the label still intact! So characteristically Russian-like!

New Merv is laid out on the usual lines which I have described in speaking of Ashkabad, much like an Indian station. Fine avenues are planted of double rows of trees, chiefly silver poplars and acacias, with a ditch of running water between, giving a cool effect which is very grateful in the sweltering months of summer when there is little to mitigate the heat. There are no punkahs, so the doors and windows of the bungalows have to be closed from eight A.M. till sunset to keep out the burning air. Ice, too, is almost unknown; indeed I have heard that its use is forbidden for fear of producing fever. Like all Russian military stations, there are no health-giving forms of exercise; drink, dancing, and card-playing seem the only diversions in vogue, and for these a casino is provided, hung with portraits of the Russian crowned heads.

A large church, with the usual five domes, ministers to their religious necessities, and a school not far off attends to the educational wants of the community. It is quite a feature in the life of Merv to see every morning bands of girls, neatly dressed with white pinafores to protect their frocks, and handkerchiefs tied over their heads, all on their way to school.

The hotel was a small one, on a scale that is known as a *nomer*, with one girl in attendance, who long before I was dressed in the morning used to dash like a whirlwind into my room, pour out showers of questions in Russian, though I was unable to reply, and swish about with a damp cloth. She surprised me one day when I paid her my washing bill by displaying a stout limb and thrusting the money into her stocking, explaining as she did so that she had no pockets.

There are no basins to empty, as throughout Central Asia in ordinary houses and inns the only washing arrangements provided are a diminutive fixed-in basin with a hole and no plug. The tiny trickle of water from a brass-spouted can hung on the wall can be turned on to spout up or to spout down, but in any case, with all one's skill, much must escape before doing more than moistening the face and hands. There are no sitting-rooms in these smaller hotels, and food is served in the bedrooms. An eatable meal was provided once a day, about noon, and to supplement this for supper I had cheese and fruit, and eggs cooked by means of a spirit-lamp – a necessary part of one's luggage. Good white bread was nearly always obtainable, and when fresh the native flat scones, called *lepeshki*, were not to be despised. Nor was even the Persian bread of muffin-like consistency (made in lengths of six or eight inches wide and sold by the yard) to be disregarded. This is an especially convenient form for such provender, as it can be rolled up and thrust into the saddle-bags in universal use on every camel, horse, or donkey back. After a few days of such treatment the teeth are to be envied that can masticate it!

The town of Merv is of importance as being the junction of a narrow-gauge railway to Khusk, on the Afghan frontier, the making of which caused some agitation in Great Britain and India, and fears were openly expressed of what Russia's further intentions might be. Lord Salisbury wrote in 1874: 'Russia must advance to Merv ultimately, and we have no power or interest to prevent it'; and again in 1880: 'Russia will be entirely unable to attack Herat until she has got the railway at least as far as Mesched; and I think I may safely put that day beyond the lifetime of this generation' – a far-seeing vision, and one that may still hold good. Peter the Great with no less astuteness records in his will: 'We must progress as much as possible in the direction of Constantinople and India. He who can once get possession of these places is the real ruler of the world.'

V

The Town of Charjui

When the mention of Khiva is made to me it is almost invariably followed by two questions: Where is it, and Why did you wish to go there? To the first I can best reply by saying that it is that district of Turkestan lying to the south of the Aral Sea, and bounded on the west by the Caspian, on the east by the Khanates of Bokhara and Kokand, with Persia lying far to the south. To the second question, I saw a more or less blank space on the map and was filled with a desire to see what lay on this seemingly nameless tract. Captain Burnaby's famous *Ride to Khiva*, in 1876, a book which made a great sensation in its day, though but little known at the present time, gives one some idea of what it is like. The knowledge of the country through which he passed has been but little increased, a country which in size is double that of Great Britain, with a native population of about a million in the Khanate.

There are three ways by which the town of Khiva can be reached. First, by riding, or driving in a camel-cart called a *telega*, across the desert from a station on the Tashkent-Orenburg Railway called Kasalinsk, where there is a ferry across the Syr Daria. Second, by following the course of the River Amu Daria on camel-back or cart from Charjui, a station on the Transcaspian Railway, some 450 miles from Khiva. Third, by boat from the same start-ing-point; which route I selected, as I heard that a small paddle steamer sailed once a fortnight for the convenience of those stationed at the military post of Petro Alexandrovsk, and there might be a chance of my being granted accommodation on board, and so achieving the journey in a space of time varying from five to twenty days. However, even with this uncertainty, it was prefer-able to a desert journey, with all the attendant discomforts of possible sandstorms, and no shelter by night except such as is afforded by the back of a recumbent camel or an upturned cart. Made roads are non-existent, as are post-houses of any kind. A railway is in contemplation on the left bank of the river. Knowing the dilatoriness of all officials in those regions in making arrange-ments, I decided to spend a few days in Charjui before starting for Khiva, and, at the same time, to see what there was of interest in the old town, distant about seven miles from the modern Russian one. This last has a certain amount of trading traffic on the River Amu Daria, near which it is built, and native boats are paddled or towed up and tap the resources of even Afghanistan, of which, in the higher reaches, it forms the frontier.

The native boats, or *caiouques* as they are called, are often of primitive construction, literally dug-outs, or else they are made of wood hollowed out by hand and caulked with mud and cotton. These are made for 100 roubles, but a Russian one costs as much as 1000 roubles. They can carry a cargo of 1000 poods, a pood being about equal to forty English pounds. They are worked by a paddle, a long-handled implement terminating in a flat heart-shaped end, which, one would imagine, could not be a very powerful means of propelling such heavy boats; but as in all Eastern doings, time is of no consideration.

Old Charjui, similar to all native towns of Central Asia, is walled round, and dominated by a citadel, which is still further protected by a wall and gates (rigidly closed at eight P.M.), and to it the inhabitants used to fly for refuge on warning being given of Turcoman raids. It is now the peaceful residence of a Beg, or governor, who administers justice in accordance with native laws and customs, and he is the chief Beg of Bokhara district. The laws the Russians have not altered, nor do they proselytize in matters of religion. After passing through one of the gates in the outer wall I met a crowd of religious devotees who, like Tommy Tucker, were busy singing for their supper, in nasal tones which reverberated through the narrow streets, and were not unlike some old Scotch psalm tune. The streets are roofed over, with the usual open-fronted shops, where eggs could be purchased for three shillings a hundred, and a special kind of marmalade made of finely chopped carrots in honey. Here and there were groves of white mulberries, whose fruit was then ripe and lay in luscious heaps all around: a superstitious fear that they cause fever forbids their consumption by the natives, but I ate freely and suffered no ill effects.

We mounted an easy flight of steps to the great door of the citadel and inside found a row of old, grey-bearded, turbaned retainers, all more or less decrepit, and in keeping with their weapons of the most primitive description which hung behind them on the wall. Such a picture might have been seen three hundred years ago, the flintlocks ending in a species of pitchfork, all interspersed with curved swords and scimitars. Having been passed on by the guard, the Beg's interpreter next appeared, a young man, a native, speaking Russian, Arabic, Afghanisky, Persian, and Sart dialects.

The day of my visit happened to fall on market day, and consequently all who had petitions to present or grievances to right swarmed up in crowds to see the Beg. I accompanied them until we reached the courtyard of the citadel, where we found the Beg seated on the floor at an open window about to open a case of horse-stealing. Grouped in front of him were the accused, the witnesses, and the owners of the horse. Officials with long wands of office made all kneel down, and showed undue partiality by cuffing the thief more than once, and violently shaking his abettor. Witnesses were encouraged to tell all they knew, and in twenty minutes the case was proved, and the owner was asked whether he would have the value of the horse or the man imprisoned. Needless to say he chose the former, and the thief was led off by the jailer to receive thirty-nine strokes with the birch-rod, or its equivalent, and be imprisoned until the sum was paid. The regulation scale is as follows: for the first theft without murder, thirty-nine strokes with the rod; for the second, seventy-five strokes and imprisonment; and for the third, the culprit is hung on market day on a gibbet, and the body left hanging for two or three days as a warning to others. By payment for the article stolen, and expenses, a thief can escape imprisonment, provided the injured party is satisfied, but he does not escape the beating. The prison is just outside the entrance to the citadel, and on entering one is led back to the Middle Ages to find men with iron collars padlocked to chains fastened to a long beam on the stone floor, and hanging outside are more chains and a heavy pointed hammer to hammer on the collars. The more unruly have, in addition, their feet in the stocks; mats are given them to sleep on, but they are not allowed out except for necessary purposes, and the only ventilation and light are from narrow slits in the wall just beneath the roof. Food is supplied by their relatives or charitably disposed persons, as none is provided, and for a small gift the prisoners bowed low and stroked down their beards, which is their polite form of expressing thanks. In the case of murder there is a regulated scale of value, 800 to 1000 roubles for a man, and about half that sum for a woman.

Turning from low to high life, I was presented to the Beg, who shook hands, and then I was ushered into a long room in the centre of which was a table laid with eighteen dishes of sweets and fancy biscuits, a special light meal, intended to do honour to a guest, called *dasturkhan*. This consisted of some sweets made of fruit, which were most acceptable, after a sketchy meal in the early morning, and even a dish of rather shrivelled Caucasus oranges was not to be despised, nor were the tumblers of pale-coloured tea. The rooms of the palace were purely Oriental in style and decoration. The walls were lined with carved and gilt wall niches like pigeon-holes, to serve the purpose of drawers or cupboards, while the floors were spread with rugs of native manufacture. The interpreter took us to his room, truly a prophet's chamber, over-looking the entrance gate, with a fine view of the city from the window, and on the low table was set a dish of *pilau*, the national food, rice cooked in mutton fat through which were scattered shreds of meat and raisins. The bowl was shared by the interpreter and my Russian servant, who scooped up balls of the mixture in their fingers with amazing rapidity. I saw there would be small chance of my getting any without the help of something more than fingers, so a battered teaspoon was found which greatly assisted, and I kept a corner of the dish to myself and partook only of the dry rice, as the bottom layer so reeked of mutton fat.

The Beg then said he would like to be photographed, and for this purpose attired himself in his best *khalat*, made of a pink and black European brocade; but not wishing this touch of vanity to

ELLA R. CHRISTIE

be made public, he seated himself in no greater prominence than at the window of his room, and I fear the result hardly did justice to the benevolent-looking old gentleman. He has also a summer palace in the town, which is a one-storey pavilion-like building, with delightful gardens and small lakes, and groves of white mulberries, the fruit of which was lying in golden heaps on the ground. Vines were rampant over the trees and pergolas, and flitting about were green parakeets and bright blue birds, said to be the blue crow, while in the evening nightingales were to be heard everywhere. Apricot-trees line the streets and the fruit is plucked for jam when about the size of a cherry, and very delicious it is.

On his victorious campaign Alexander the Great crossed the Oxus at Charjui, where is now an iron-girder railway bridge over a mile in length, which forms an imposing feature in the landscape, and of which I was to get a still better idea on the day that I left in the steamer for Khiva.

VI

The Journey to Khiva from Charjui

Washing Arrangements – Life on the Amu Daria – Sandstorm – Mennonites – Caiouques and Carts – Bahai Disciples

The day of departure for Khiva at length arrived, and as the boat left at eight A.M. I spent the previous night on board: a cabin had been reserved for me, thanks to the kindness of Romanoffsky of the Russian agency at Bokhara. The starting-point of the boat is about one and a half miles from the railway station of Charjui, and to reach it one had to plough through an expanse of dust.

The steamers are entirely military ones, and the officers have a prior claim to the five cabins, which offer no luxuries, and in which there are no berths, merely a broad shelf on which to lay one's rug and cushion; while washing arrangements are confined to a small metal can with a spout at the bottom which hangs outside the saloon and allows water to escape almost drop by drop into the palms of one's hands. One morning I asked for a pail of the river water, but had one used it one might as well have taken a mud-bath. There was a small saloon, or 'cuddy,' for that just describes it, which was overcrowded with twelve passengers, and at times it was suffocatingly hot. A meal was usually served about twelve A.M. and another at seven-thirty P.M., while the hours between were occupied by the Russians in drinking countless tumblers of tea and in endless talk. I used to wonder if their own proverb ever came into their minds: 'The tongue has no bones yet it can break bones.' The menu for the first day's dinner was as follows: mutton broth, boiled sturgeon with pickles, and a so-called plum pudding; while the supper consisted of sausages and apples.

I was early awakened by the tramp of what seemed regiments of men; in reality I suppose there was only one. Each spare inch of the boat was occupied; there was no steerage provision, so the natives lay on every vacant corner, a double row of them round the outside of the saloon, while on both paddle-boxes there was a fine encampment of Turcomans, Kirghiz, and Sarts; some of them had bundles and felt rugs – these last stamped in patterns of red, blue, and brown – while others were the proud possessors of *pushtins* or Afghan fur-lined coats, and enviable rugs and saddle-bags, not omitting to mention the native pipe or *chilim*, one of which had the ashes retained by a bit of old chain armour. The deck was laid with metal plates nailed down, so no scrubbing was necessary; indeed it would have been impossible owing to the crowded state of the boat. We started off in fine style, but in a quarter of an hour the bow was firmly wedged into the bank. I should have thought that in spite of a strong current this could have been avoided, and it took us two hours to get off, thanks to poling and punting and shoving by the soldiers. I afterwards found this was our daily rate of progression, as we seldom did more than ten minutes to half-an-hour without this happening. The river is nevertheless worthy of the encomium passed upon it by the late Lord Curzon in his book on Central Asia. He says:

'The Gihon of Eden, that encompasseth the whole land of Ethiopia, the Vak-Shu of Sanscrit literature, the Oxus of the Greeks, the Amu Daria, or River Sen of the Tatars, no river, not even the Nile, can claim a nobler tradition or a more illustrious history. Descending from the hidden Roof of the World, its waters tell of forgotten peoples and whisper secrets of unknown lands. They are believed to have reached the cradle of our race. Long the legendary water-mark between Iran and Turan, they have worn a channel deep into the fate of humanity. World-wide conquerors, an Alexander and a Tamerlane, slaked their horses' thirst in the Oxus stream; Eastern poets drank inspiration from its fountains; Arab geographers boasted of it as superior in volume, in depth, and in breadth to all the rivers of the earth.'

The River Amu Daria, or ancient Oxus, rises in the Pamirs, and after a course of 1500 miles is discharged by several mouths into the Aral Sea. The water begins to rise in April and is at its lowest in November. In parts it is wide, almost like an inland sea, but without enormous expense will never be of much use for navigation because of the heavy deposit which is carried down. In some winters it is frozen as far south as Charjui, the ice melting by the end of January. The water was so shallow that constant soundings with a pole had to be taken. The boat could draw 3½ feet of water, but as a rule the pole showed 4 feet; 140 feet is its greatest depth.

Matthew Arnold in his inimitable language thus describes the course of the Oxus:

> But the majestic river floated on
> Out of the mist and hum of the lowland,
> Into the frosty starlight, and there moved
> Rejoicing, through the hushed Chorasmian waste
> Under the solitary moon: he flow'd
> Right for the Polar Star, past Orinje,
> Brimming, and bright, and large: then sands begin
> To hem his watery march, and dam his streams,

And split his currents; that for many a league,
The shorn and parcell'd Oxus strains along
Through beds of sand and matted rushy isles –
Oxus, forgetting the bright speed he had
In his high mountain cradle in Pamere,
A foil'd circuitous wanderer: till at last
The long'd for dash of waves is heard, and wide
His luminous home of waters opens, bright
And tranquil, from whose floor the new bath'd stars
Emerge, and shine upon the Aral Sea.

We had on board the new commandant of the district of Khiva and his wife, going to Petro Alexandrovsk, he much medalled, and speaking a little French, but his wife Russian only. We tied up every evening about seven-thirty, owing to navigation difficulties, and in my mind one unforgettable picture remains of a village with its lights twinkling like glow-worms and a fleet of boats resting on the water like giant white moths. A sandstorm was a less pleasant experience. One calm sunny morning I saw in the distance what looked like a genuine Scotch mist; suddenly it was upon us, and for hours a hot wind blew, carrying with it a suffocating cloud of sand. We had to tie up, every crevice was closed that was possible; the steerage passengers lay face downwards as flat on the deck as space would permit, their bodies and even their heads rolled in *khalats* and blankets to try to keep out the atmosphere that would choke them if breathed directly. Towards evening it was past, but I thought we should never get rid of the sand that lay thick in the closed cabins.

Soon after leaving Charjui we passed a range of square-looking, flat-topped hills, or perhaps they are better described as high mounds, which tradition declares to be the bones of the horse of the prophet Elijah. The prophet leaped on horseback across the river to convert the natives to Mohammedanism, and as he did so the dust rose on the opposite side where he landed and left a permanent memorial of his missionary journey.

Away from earth he travelled; yet he somehow seemed to know
The road, as if his weary steps had trod it long ago:
And was not that the wilderness, to which he once had fled?
And that the lonely juniper where he had wished him dead?

And was not that the cave where he had sat in sullen mood,
Until he heard the still small voice that touched his heart with good?
And was not that the road by which from Carmel he had run
Before the chariot of the king about the set of sun?

There is not much cultivation until reaching Tonya Myonu, meaning 'the camel's rest,' and at that spot the telegraph wire crosses the river. On the left bank there is a thick scrub of willow, poplar, birch, prickly acacia with thorns five to six inches long, tamarisk, and a willow-looking silvery leafed tree known as the *djidda*, that gives out an aromatic perfume when crushed, tall reeds and grasses with an undergrowth of liquorice. In this jungle may be found wild boar, deer of various species, wolves, and, farther east, leopards and tigers. The shores are the home of countless varieties of birds: wild geese, black eagle, wagtails of different kinds, pigeons, blue crow, yellow oriole, and many others. The right bank is an absolute desert, though remnants of mud-houses are still to be seen, bearing out the tradition that before the devastating raids of Ginghiz Khan took place, that side was so thickly populated that a cat could leap from house to house along that now desolate shore.

When we stopped, all the steerage passengers swarmed out to cook their evening meal; several seemed to club together in order to prepare it and then consume the large bowls of *pilau*, while also sharing a *chilim*, and these little chattering groups round the fire seemed to eat half the night.

A halt of two hours made a little diversion at a place called Darganata, some three miles off, but one could see its old walls rising above the thickets of willows and tall reeds. The paddle steamer was hauled up on to the edge of the bank and tethered in the jungle, where there was not even a sign of any landing-place. A lighter was there to pump in oil, and it took off a sack of meat and a heap of what I thought were patent bricks, till I was told they were bread for the military! No attempt was made to keep them free of dust or dirt. Later in my journey I met them again in the form of crusts being taken in truckloads to make *kvass*, the favourite Russian drink.

We had on board two Mennonites who belonged to a colony near Khiva, Christians of a very austere kind. I do not know if they approved of conversation or not, but one said he would answer any questions I liked to ask him, but in the way of conversation one could go little further. They are German-speaking in the form of Plattdeutsch, and the sect is called Mennonite after Simon Menno, the founder of the later school of Anabaptists in Holland. He was born in 1496, and officiated for some years as a priest, but finally from conviction left the Romish church: he gathered a considerable following, who settled first in Russia, and their chief tenets now appear to be – objection to military service, refusal to serve in any capacity under any government they consider non-Christian, and the practice of adult baptism. They are opposed to vaccination. They have no ordained clergy, but a leader is chosen in a colony to direct spiritual and temporal matters.

When military service was made compulsory in Prussia they migrated to the Crimea and districts near the Volga. In 1880 some Mennonites of the latter colonies got carried away by the fanaticism of one of their number, who vowed that he had received orders from on high to proceed to Turkestan. The party disagreed as to the ultimate destination, and so divided, one going to Aulieata, and the other to a spot nine miles from Khiva; in both places they have prosperous colonies, and in the latter district have reclaimed from the salt marshes large tracts of land now well cultivated.

Before leaving the boat the captain tried to make difficulties about my permit; luckily I had a letter from the British Embassy, but as he knew no English the General's card commending me to the kind offices of the Russians in Khiva had more weight, and for two roubles he agreed to give me a paper duly filled up. The General's French acquired greater fluency on the voyage as at our table of six I sat on one side of him and he daily limped along in his halting speech. His wife sat on his other side, and with three officers who talked Russian all the time our number was complete. The other tables were reserved for Urgentsch commercial travellers, who listened with bated breath to the words that dropped from the *haut ton*, but they did not venture to join in the conversation. The manners of all left much to be desired, salt was scooped up with their knives and bread speared on their forks, while the General and his wife shared each other's dishes and tumbler.

The journey was accomplished well within a week, but never was an arrival less welcomed. At six-thirty P.M. the boat drew up on the blank shore of a vast desert expanse, without a stick or stone to mark the landing. A native *caiouque*, or boat, was in waiting, with two or three natives ready to take off the passengers. The

General remarked: '*C'est comme Paradis.*' Anything more unlike what one has been taught to imagine Paradise to be, it would be hard to find. I suppose I looked for an explanation, for he said slowly: '*Parce qu'il n'y a pas des maisons.*' The natives all swarmed out with their bundles into the *caiouque*, but I felt that if I had to remain for ever nothing would induce me to go with that crowd, and night approaching. I was further discouraged, if that was possible, by the General pointing out the *chef des caiouques*, a wild-looking Khivan, who volunteered the information that another *caiouque* could come the following morning. I was thus left with the Mennonites and commercials, who all wished to start at three A.M. in order to reach Novi Urgentsch, our first stopping-place, before twelve, but I shall always feel glad to have seen the picturesque departure of the first *caiouque* sailing off into the sunset not unlike some Viking ship of old.

The next excitement was the departure of the General. Two amazing carriages, such as could only be produced in Russia, dashed up with three mounted guards. The General and his wife occupied one, which literally was about the size of a modern perambulator, while the maid and officer got into the other, and off they all galloped across the reedy ground, which was destitute of even a track. I still marvel how they escaped being thrown out, as that species of carriage has neither sides nor back. No one seemed to mind, not even the General's wife, a lady of a certain age, who wore a brown sailor hat and was said to be a martyr to indigestion. Before starting next morning at five-thirty the captain took a photograph of me as being the first Englishwoman to go to Khiva. Along with us on the *caiouque* were a few natives, a Tatar, two Russian traders, the two Mennonites, and my servant. We left before sunrise, 'and the first grey of morning filled the east, and the fog rose out of the Oxus stream.' That sight I shall never forget – of a grey dusk, and then the sun as it rose lighting up the faces of our strange Turcoman crew in their dark red *khalats* and black sheepskin busbies. Their robes were girdled by waist-belts of embroidered bath towels and checked house dusters, while they refreshed themselves frequently with straw-coloured tea out of handleless cups, which when empty they thrust into the folds of their robes, and sucked green snuff out of their gourd snuff bottles, which is the Turcoman form of enjoying tobacco. The *caiouque*, with its mascot of horsehair at the prow, was not uncomfortable, though dusty to a degree, owing to its being daubed inside with mud instead of pitch, but rugs were spread and we sat upon our luggage. Three men paddled with what I can only describe as long-handled butter-pats, and a loop of rope was used instead of a rowlock; they may have tried to keep time but utterly failed to do so, and it was thanks to the stream, which carried us along at quite a fast rate, that after two hours on the river we entered the canal which leads to Novi Urgentsch.

The canal was crossed at frequent intervals by trestle bridges, devoid of parapets of any kind, of fragile construction, which were never repaired till someone fell through. Poplar sticks were laid along the supports, and these were then covered over with stones and turf sods; none too wide for wheeled traffic, they certainly did not allow space for a skittish horse, so prudence always said to me 'Get down' when on future occasions our road led us by such danger tracks.

Along the sides of both river and canal are water-wheels, called *shigeer*, for irrigation purposes. These are turned by camels, oxen, horses, and donkeys blindfolded, as they are driven round and round in a very narrow circle. The creak of the wheel and the swish of the water as each jar empties itself into the ditch made to carry it to the land are unforgettable sounds. Some wheels are of double construction, and are driven in this case by the river current. All this irrigation is native planned, but the Russian Government had shortly before sent one of their officers to study such work in India. Nothing can be grown in Turkestan except by such artificial means, and where carried out the desert can indeed be made to blossom as the rose.

The *caiouque* journey being ended, there still remained some miles to be covered by cart before we reached Novi Urgentsch. These native carts, or *arbas*, are strongly built, and have enormous wheels, five to seven feet in diameter, in order to negotiate mud-holes; they have broad wooden spokes, and no iron rims, but instead are heavily iron-studded, and of course there are no springs, so the jolting sensation on these high raised studs may be better imagined than described. In addition, a ladder is almost required by which to ascend to the body of the cart, as the shaft is set so high. I started by walking, but eventually dust and distance overcame my decision to go on foot, and clambering up by the spokes I entered Novi Urgentsch in proper style.

On arrival there I was told by the Russian authorities to ask for the house of the Khan of Khiva's Minister of Finance, Buchaloff by name, who would provide accommodation, as there are no inns of any kind. Unfortunately he was from home. His nephew and three or four other natives were seated on the floor of a windowless room, around a fire sunk in the floor, and waiting, like Micawber, for something to turn up. They had no power to grant accommodation in the absence of the Minister at Khiva, and darkness had nearly fallen before I at length found a room in what was called the *Cloob*! This consisted of a music hall, a room for meals, and a small room opening off it stored with bottles and rubbish of all kinds. This was cleared out (the footlights being left) and I installed myself and camp-bed, and a table and chair were provided. Such a strange odour pervaded the place that I had to send Fritz for a disinfectant and sprayed it all thoroughly. There was no fastening of any kind to the door, so I insisted on a nail and piece of string. Fritz got housed with a Russian family, who obligingly shared their room with him.

The mud walls which once surrounded Novi Urgentsch are now partially destroyed; its native quarter consists of the usual mud-built houses, with a raised platform in front, upon which the owner spends the greater part of the day, either for pleasure or business. The Russian quarter consists of wooden houses, with a bank, the Russo-Asiatic Bank, with its German manager, a post and telegraph office, a church and European store.

Novi Urgentsch is the centre of the cotton trade, in the district of Khiva, and has two market days in the week, Sunday and Thursday, on which days only are the shops open, when samples of most of the Khivan tribes are to be met with, and strings of those imposing-looking Bactrian camels, very often led by a diminutive donkey.

Whilst prowling round the town I came on a burying-ground. Bodies are buried sitting, with gourds and such-like personal possessions beside them; a small house of poplar sticks and mud is then built over them. This in time, of course, disintegrates, and skulls and bones were lying about in all directions, where animals had intruded.

One walk brought another strange experience, though this time of a pleasanter nature. I found a group seated on a rug playing cards; one of them was our Persian fellow-passenger of the boat, and he explained his host was a dealer in carpets and tea (but I found everyone in Novi Urgentsch dealt in something, or else his house served as a depot for stores). This led to some trivial conversation, and I left, to be overtaken by one of the group, who begged me to come into his house, as he had some English publications to show me. Curious to see what they were, I found them to be *The Star of the East*, the American publication of the sect of the Bahais. He was overjoyed to find anyone who had ever heard of the name, wrung my hand, and presented me with a charming little purse of native make as a remembrance 'from the East to the West.' Curiously enough, the day happened to be the birthday of Abdul Bahai, the leader of the sect, which is regarded as a festival, so the table was set out with tea and sweetmeats, and the Persian and another Bahai were celebrating it alone in that remote region.

As a further remembrance they gave me their rosaries, made, they said, of jade from Afghanistan. One is curiously like a yellow stone found in parts of Baltistan and there made into bowls and cups; the other of a dark green semi-opaque stone which was quite new to me.

Some of the houses have lovely old pillars carved at the foot in an ascending design, supporting balconies; or, if the pillars be not carved, they are painted in red, blue, green and white encircling lines.

Before leaving Novi Urgentsch I called on Buchaloff, and found him to be an imposing-looking person, clad in a dark-red-and-green-striped silk *khalat*, with a mixed yellow and purple shawl tied round his waist: he invited me to share a seat on a rug, and offered hospitality on my return journey from Khiva. Conversation flagged, and I left after a mutual expression of hoping to meet there, for which journey, he said, the Beg, the local governor, would provide a carriage. I do not know whether *indirectly* the Beg provided the droshky, but *directly* it was procured for me by a trader who refused payment for the use of it. It was literally a basket on wheels, and incapable of carrying any luggage, so mine had to be sent off early in an *arba*. The forty versts were driven in four hours' time across desert strips, where, luckily, rain had fallen the previous evening and freshened the wonderful colouring of the oases through which we passed, till at length Khiva appeared in sight.

VII

Life in Khiva

*A Haven of Refuge – A Bad Stube – A Minister's
Reception – Mennonite Colony – A Supper-
Party – The Khan and his Cavalcade*

Lines of green and gold, and gold and green, beyond which the
walls and minarets of Khiva appeared in sight. Can that be really
Khiva? I was forced to say. The scene filled one with a thrill of
satisfaction. All past difficulties and discomforts were forgotten,
and future ones unthought of – the goal was reached. As we neared
the town, a building, whose foundations were little more than
laid, showed itself just outside one of the gates. Anything of a
modern nature seemed so surprising – its purpose, as I afterwards
learned, not less so, being a post office and fever hospital combined;
surely an absolutely unique arrangement either in the history of
post offices or hospitals. There were no postal arrangements of any
kind, nor of course a telegraph, yet that town of 60,000 inhabitants seemed to have prospered notwithstanding its lack of either.
Letters, should anyone ever be seized with the extraordinary desire
to write, or to have recourse to the professional letter-writers,
must be handed over to the care of someone attending the market
at Novi Urgentsch. This has to be done on Thursday for Sunday's
mail, with all the accompanying risks of being lost *en route*. If it

did reach Novi Urgentsch it might lie there, as the postman frequently laid letters aside from one mail to another, there being only two in the week to Charjui. As to delivery, I imagine the same course was followed, and a chance visitor to the post office or town was entrusted with anything for Khiva. I had a letter to Colonel Korniloff, the Russian advisor to the Khan, so went first to his house to see about accommodation, as there was not even a possible inn or native *serai*.

Colonel Korniloff's house, though mud-built, was on European lines, and looked so clean and comfortable that I longed to stay, but he said rooms for strangers were to be had at the palace of the Khan, the native ruler of the country, and he would go there in two hours, as the Khan was then asleep, and ask permission for me to be entertained. Meantime his hospitable wife bustled about for my comfort, and having to deal with a lady who had come all the way from Petrograd, she felt nothing less than scent could be offered with which to wash her face. Two bottles, one stronger in perfume than the other, were brought, as well as a box of powder; then a meal, which was even more acceptable, was served at four P.M., tea with rusks and excellent ham and jam; and how good it all tasted after a fast since breakfast at eight A.M.

About five P.M. Korniloff said the Khan would now be awake, so he clad himself in his becoming grey uniform, medals and all, buckled on his sword and set off in his droshky to ask the requisite permission of the Khan. Apparently my arrival had caused some perturbation, as never before had there been a woman traveller to cater for, and the problem was where to put her; not quite *comme il faut* in the palace, and yet hospitality had to be maintained. In two hours Korniloff returned, to my intense relief saying that the Khan thought that I had better stay where I was; so rooms were arranged for myself and Fritz, as I was obliged to keep him at hand to interpret, for neither Korniloff nor his wife spoke a word of anything but Russian and Khivan, and my Russian was very limited. Almost the first question she asked me was, what was my father's name. This seemed odd, but I found it was in order that she might address me in proper fashion as Ella Ivanovna – Ella, the daughter of John – and she signified she was Natalia Anatolia; rather a mouthful, so in these pages she is known as 'Natalia An.'

I was next informed there was a *bad stube*, for which I wrung her hands in gratitude, somewhat diminished when I found I was expected to share it with the whole family. The *bad stube* was lighted only twice a week at four P.M., and this was one of the days. It seemed too short an acquaintance to be on such familiar terms as to share a bath with all the party, so I explained I never could take one except immediately after a meal, and this I knew would not meet with the approval of the Russians, who eat not merely heartily but enormously. The suggestion seemed to put her out dreadfully. However, it was finally arranged that the stove should be kept up longer, and in spite of a large meal of soup, meat and sweets at seven o'clock, I accompanied her afterwards to the yard at the back of the house. Suitable bathing attire not forming part of my travelling kit, my mind wavered between a nightgown or a Burberry, and finally the latter carried the day. She was a most motherly person, whose family of twelve children, luckily for me, were all out in the world, and she felt it her duty to superintend the bathing function. We entered a covered shed where the stove was burning, and here she poured volumes of water on the floor to raise the steam. On one side of the shed were three raised benches, and on the other side a single one; on one end of this were laid a large brass basin filled with water, bunches of fibre, three cakes of soap and three eggs. My heart rather sank at the idea that it was considered necessary to remain long enough in the bath to require further nourishment after the excellent meal which we had just taken. But I said nothing, and after many explanations in Russian the good lady was induced at last to leave me, though she twice returned to see how I was getting on.

The luxury of having unlimited water that one could use was delightful, after weeks of stinted quantities boiled in samovars or in a travelling saucepan. I bathed and dried, and then remembered the can of hot water, with which all was to be finished, so I had to begin it all over again, and once more my hostess appeared (there was not even a bit of string with which to fasten the door), and sighed and groaned, and wrung her hands. I did not know what I had done, or left undone, but she was only appeased when she saw me safely tucked up in bed, and compelled me to drink a glass of tea in which was stirred a generous helping of cherry jam.

A peaceful sleep followed this day of novel experiences, and at by no means an early hour I was awakened, ready to start afresh. Tea and rusks began the day. These rusks are much in use, being merely slices of bread dried in the oven, and are a convenient form of using up stale bread. The midday meal began with ham and sardines; then followed the soup, with about a pound of meat, out of which the soup had been made, in each plate; the soup was taken first, and then the meat was eaten with mustard. Another meat course followed, and finally a sweet – *kissel*, a fruit jelly which was often served, was a favourite dish. The meal was washed down with excellent home-made white wine and tumblers and tumblers of tea after to finish off. Indeed, the tea-drinking used to go on until four o'clock.

In return for lessons in Russian dishes I offered to make an English dish, the only one I felt competent to tackle with success being scrambled eggs. Knowing the appetites I had to deal with, I made a supply that would have sufficed for more than double the number in England, but the only remark I elicited was from Korniloff, who appropriated it all, and observed that 'it might be very good for people who had no teeth.'

Colonel Korniloff spent a whole afternoon showing me everything of interest. In the town and everywhere our visit caused crowds to assemble, so that the chief outrider had to keep them in order by means of a short-handled whip with a fringed lash. We met Natalia An. in the bazaar on our return, and we had quite a gay procession home: first the outriders, and a species of foxhound we had picked up on the way; then Natalia An. and myself in our carriage, which was practically only a basket set on wheels, without sides or back to it, as the seat was laid across. Her arm was tucked affectionately in mine, and her head was enveloped in a yellow shawl. Korniloff and Fritz brought up the rear in the other basket. Natalia An.'s occupations were endless. She did a great part of the cooking, baking, and roasting on paraffin stoves; the roasting was done in cast-iron covered dishes, and with excellent results.

As to the beds, there were no blankets, but native silk-covered quilts filled with camel wool took their place, and anything more delightfully warm and light could not be imagined. All the bed linen was trimmed with the finest crochet lace, the work of the clever and industrious fingers of Natalia An., and the triumph of it in her eyes was holding it up to the light 'just like machine.' There was one house servant, Solai by name, the son of a mullah (priest); he used to wear a fine gold brocade skull-cap, and slipped about in bare feet, well aware of the dignity of his social position. Being sent one day to market, he was seen by Natalia An. returning on a donkey, and on her asking the reason of this extravagance, he said: 'Should I, son of a mullah, be seen carrying home a cabbage on foot?' This dignity had a sad fall. Desirous of seeing life, the son of a mullah saw too much in an adventure of three days, and to clear his gambling debts then incurred his wages were docked weekly by his master.

Having received information that the Khan's minister, Islam Hodja, wished to receive me, Colonel Korniloff and I, with Fritz in attendance, set off one morning in the victoria, his best carriage, built in Kasan (where there is a celebrated maker). His palace is not far from the Khan's summer one. We drew up at a courtyard, where were tethered a number of horses, all of them overlaid with gay trappings of various kinds, and embroidered rugs that covered them from eyes to tail.

Several courts had to be traversed, some with trees and one with a raised flat stone fireplace in the centre, while at least twelve retainers hung around. At length the great man's veranda was reached. The veranda was supported on carved pillars, and in it were chairs, a painted oval garden seat and a table. Islam Hodja, a tall, fine-looking man in silk robes, rose with great dignity, shook hands and placed me beside him on the garden seat, while tea in tumblers, with sweetmeats and fancy biscuits, was at once offered. I conversed by means of Fritz, who interpreted that the Khan wished to present me with a portrait of himself, and then Islam Hodja gave me one of himself. These I asked him to sign, which he did, in Persian characters, and his own bore the inscription that it was presented to 'Ella Hristie' at Khiva, and the date. He also gave me an ancient Khivan gold coin, the date uncertain, though said to be of the eleventh century. He next asked if I would like to see his rooms, as he evidently was very proud of their European furnishings. In the first saloon was a grand piano, which of course no one could play, and it was merely there as an ornament. The rest of the room was filled with a suite of bronzed and gilt chairs covered in royal blue plush, mirrors and china vases, all in execrable taste, while the parquet floor was not even disguised with any of the native rugs, which are always attractive.

The second saloon was the winter one, decorated with quite attractive native plaster-work, and had a carved and gilt cornice. The ceiling was painted blue, and the room furnishing consisted of a small low table, two mirrors and an appalling gilt chandelier. My host seemed a most intelligent man, and one who could be interested in Western ideas – perhaps too much so, as he was virtually the ruler, and his sad fate is described in a later chapter.

Having expressed a wish to visit the Mennonite colony at Ach Meshed, some nine miles from Khiva, Natalia An. said nothing could be better, as she had a dear friend there whom she had not seen for nine years. She and I started in the clothes-basket droshky, and were driven by Solai, as the coachman had suddenly decamped, which, apparently, is quite a common occurrence with the native servants. There are no made roads anywhere, so he and his mistress argued all the time which was the best track to follow, and I do think, out of sheer cussedness, when she said one track he said another, and in most cases it was a worse one. We had one horse harnessed to the shafts, and on the right side was a spare one tied on in the usual negligent way, which allowed it to gallop all over the place, and I vowed inwardly that Natalia An. should have that seat and the chances of its heels on the return journey.

After one and a half hour's jolting we arrived at the colony, consisting of 140 families, and went first to the home of Madame von Riesen, Natalia An.'s friend, a pleasant, refined-looking woman. My friend of the boat, Otto Toens, having heard of our arrival, next appeared and took us to his house, where we were refreshed with excellent home-made bread and butter and wine, a product also of the colony. Not a ripple from the outer world disturbed the peace of its atmosphere: not a book even was visible except in the von Riesens' home, and the offer to send any was simply not accepted. The houses were mud-built, but spotlessly clean and comfortable, thanks to the care of the sad-faced-looking women sewing at their doors, their hair brushed so smoothly as not even to allow a frisky curl to escape; and, to add a further solemnity to their appearance, they were clad in black skirts, with black and white bodices, even colours being forbidden.

The colony had been in existence for twenty-eight years, and in that time had entirely reclaimed its land from the salt marshes, the only tax levied being twelve to thirteen roubles per annum on one and a quarter acres. There was a carpenter's workshop, where new doors for the Khan's palace were being made, and also wooden flower-pots for his courtyards, which, unlike the other sober colouring of the colony, were being painted blue, yellow and red, while wooden troughs and pipes designed for a fresh-water supply were being ingeniously hollowed out of the trunks of trees, exactly as were those in use in our country four hundred years ago. Turcomans were employed at this work, and were paid forty to eighty kopecks (9d. to 1s. 3d.) a day, with food. There was a school with about twenty scholars, seated on little rough-looking wooden benches, which were all they were allowed, no such luxury as desks even being permitted, and at the time of my visit the authorities were trying to find a teacher. Mr Otto Toens had recently purchased a harmonium, which he asked me to try, as his knowledge of such instruments seemed very vague, producing for the purpose the only music he had, a copy of Sankey's hymns in German. I gave a performance with such marked acceptation to the company that I was promptly offered the post of teacher and organist to the colony for life. Many were the persuasions: 'You like our colony, why will you not always remain with us?' I felt that I could never make a good Mennonite, so I had to decline the

proposal. A cottage had even been prepared as a further induce-
ment, and disappointment was openly expressed that their efforts
had been in vain!

A shop is run for the colony where most necessaries can be
purchased, and I treasure a delightful pair of stockings softer than
the finest Shetland, made from the inner hair of the goat. If only
the feet of the colony ladies had been a little smaller!

In the upheaval of the world's catastrophe one often wonders
how it fared with the colony. Was it still a haven of peace or a
harbour of war? Did it forsake the Fatherland and uphold the
Tsar, or did the inhabitants live on in blissful ignorance of those
events that might prove to be their undoing? Whatever their
circumstances, we may be certain of this – that the Bolshevist
wave must have rudely disturbed the placid surface of existence in
that islet of industry in the salt marshes of the Amu Daria.

When we returned home the *bad stube* was in full blast, but we
were spared the company of Korniloff, as he had had the first 'go'
before our arrival, while at supper all congratulated themselves on
their feeling of comfort and being so clean after such a thorough
washing, and certainly the transformation in my host and hostess
was wonderful.

One evening we were invited to supper with a watch-maker of
German extraction and his wife, a Russian, holding the official
position of *sage femme* to the Court. Natalia An. explained before-
hand that the rooms were not large, so as to prepare me for a
house in the bazaars, as distinctive from her house, which stood in
its own grounds. The front part was a shop, and off that was the
dwelling-house. The room into which we were shown had one
half spread with the regulation gaudily flowered Russian carpet,
and the other half was occupied by a tea-table, and round the
room was the usual formal row of chairs. The hostess, speaking

only Russian, greeted us warmly and begged us to be seated at the tea-table. Her appearance would have made a fortune on any stage – a scraggy, comic face, in resemblance something between Grossmith and Dan Leno, with her wisp of hair tightly screwed into a little knot. Between refreshments she smoked cigarettes and picked her teeth with a match. Tea was served in two samovars, an allowance of three tumblers being given to each person. It was drunk very slowly, so that they took an hour and a half to consume, while a brisk conversation was kept up between the two ladies, who talked louder and louder to me, as if by this means they could make me understand what was perfectly unintelligible, the numbers at lotto – Korniloff's favourite game, which we played every evening – being about my limit.

I then thought we would leave, but Natalia An. sat glued to her chair, while the hostess washed all the glasses and spoons and placed the sweets in an adjoining bedroom, out of which she brought plates, knives and forks, dusting every one scrupulously before she set them before us. The husband arrived with the tea, a glum-looking German, suffering from asthma; he slightly thawed when he found I knew Dr Lansdell, who had stayed with him at Kuldja, adding that he was *'ein grosser reiser, aber ein grösser lüger!'* (he was 'a great traveller, but a greater story-teller!'). Before leaving home Dr Lansdell very kindly gave me much useful information for my projected visit to Central Asia, and on saying good-bye he pressed a small volume into my hand, adding: 'You will require some reading matter for your journey.' What was my surprise to find that it was a copy of his own work, *The Tithe in Scripture* – hardly suitable as a guide-book to Central Asia, or even as appropriate reading when there!

The table was covered with the usual white-wax-cloth in imitation of damask, as in Central Asia one never sees the real article, and the substitute is so much more practical for conditions of life there. Dishes were brought in of sliced sausage, smoked herring decked with slices of hard-boiled eggs and rings of onions, and a dish of sliced cheese, followed by roast chicken with pickled fungus, and salad of *Sauerkraut* and grapes. Once more the sweets were produced from the bedroom, with another samovar and another 'service' of tea, which lasted until eleven P.M., by which time I was more than exhausted – the result of a walk round the city walls and hearing the constant talk in Russian, with the exception of spasmodic conversation with my host.

The drive home by moonlight was truly lovely, the minarets and poplars standing out so clearly against the dark blue sky; and dashing through the mysterious darkness of the bazaars one barely avoided an occasional figure curled up fast asleep, pointed out as a watcher, though occasionally the beat of a drum was to be heard, showing that at least someone was awake. An oil-lamp was hung at long intervals, and of course the droshky was innocent of lamps.

I had the chance one day of seeing the Khan riding to his palace, followed by all his ministers, and a species of foot-guard in attendance, boys in long red coats, each carrying a battle-axe over one shoulder. I quite felt a link with the upper ten of Khiva when I was saluted by the two ministers, Islam Hodja and Buchaloff, the Minister of Finance. The only other occasion of my meeting the latter was some weeks later in Moscow. A rather shabby-looking spare figure, in a tight-fitting long black alpaca coat, and a close-fitting bowl-like hat almost devoid of brim, on a small-shaped head, rushed up to me and shook hands effusively, evidently delighted, when so far from home, to meet anyone he recognized. For the moment my memory failed me, until Fritz luckily came to the rescue and named him. Away from his mutton *pilaus*, he looked starved and home-sick, and with joy he mentioned that he was returning the following week. Truly 'fine feathers make fine birds,' his rich *khalats* and caracul cap having been discarded in favour of what he doubtless thought was a fashionable attire, but with them he lost even the semblance of the dignity that had been such a pronounced feature in his progress through Khiva.

The present Khan is an Uzbeg, a weak-looking specimen, the youngest of seven sons, and of his family of eighteen children only four survive. His name is Said Esphanzir Bagadour (mighty) Khan, a fine name for such a measly-looking man.

After a week of great kindness I had at length to say farewell to my hospitable friends, and their orchard with its singing birds. Natalia An. looked quite sad as we left, and, as parting gifts for the journey, she gave me a bag of loaves, a fruit-cake, a box of dried pickled cabbage and a bag of camel wool. Kind Natalia An., who could then have dreamt of such a fate awaiting you?

VIII

Khiva & the Khanate

Bazaars of Khiva – Palaces and Prisons – Mosques and Medresses – Children – Farm Buildings – Kirghiz

The town of Khiva is situated 293 feet above sea-level, and was made the capital of the Khanate on the destruction of Novi Urgentsch by Ginghiz Khan in 1219. It is still as remote and as difficult of access as when Captain Burnaby travelled there in 1876, in spite of his optimistic remark that, 'should the Russian Government ever permit Englishmen to travel in their Asiatic dominions, Khiva will probably become known to Mr Cook and on the list of his personally conducted tours.' His stay in Khiva lasted only some forty-eight hours, when he was suddenly recalled by the War Office.

The town is surrounded by double mud walls, the outer one measuring some four miles, completely encircled by a ditch now partially overgrown with reeds, while the inner or citadel wall is of oval form, seven hundred yards long by five hundred and forty broad. These walls, built of sun-dried brick plastered over with mud, are wide at the bottom, tapering up to about six feet at the top, and strengthened where necessary by buttresses and towers. They are said to have been built by Allah Kuli Elan in 1840, but were then, more probably, only restored, and as a modern defence they are useless. Access is gained by eight gates in the outer wall, which are all barred at eight P.M., as are also the four gates in the citadel wall. On the slope, where the soil in course of time has been washed down, is a collection of casket-like mounds, a convenient resting-place for defunct Khivans, so that the citadel slope has virtually become a burying-place. There are no properly made roads or streets in the town, and some of them are mere tracks and are really meant only for riding. This is the usual form in which the traffic is conducted, but so narrow are the streets that a heavily charged camel has difficulty sometimes in passing along. The bazaars, with their open-fronted shops, are roofed with boards which are covered with mats that leak freely in wet weather, and as the roadway is of a particularly greasy mud, walking is perilous; but then no one in Khiva, unless the veriest beggar, does walk. There is a choice of camel, horse or donkey back, and a few droshkys are available if specially ordered, as well as native carts. The *multum in parvo* vehicle is unknown on the ways of Khiva.

The bazaars are most attractive from the colouring and picturesqueness of the crowds; and where else in a town could one see, on peeping in at a door, a blindfolded camel patiently plodding round and round, turning a mill for grinding corn? By the same method oil is extracted from linseed. In dry weather the dust is as unpleasant as the mud after rain, and no means are in use for allaying it beyond an occasional ladleful of water, scooped by some householder out of the attractive large blue and green jars that are part of the furnishing of most courtyards. Sometimes when these jars are no longer fit to hold water the bottoms are knocked out and they are then inverted and used as chimneys, which gives a unique effect to the flat roofs.

In the bazaars one can sometimes find really good rugs and saddle-bags, and the moment a rumour goes round that such are being looked for, a most varied assortment of good, bad and indifferent are produced for inspection. Caracul skins can also be found, though it is not really the country for that breed of sheep, and the number to be found there is limited. Some silk is woven, and the colours of red and green are good, not being aniline dyes, while those used as waist-cloths are like rainbow flashes, so wonderfully blended are the colours.

There are silversmiths at work with primitive appliances, crucibles of stone heated on charcoal fires, and not much stock on hand, the usual method being for the customer to take the metal, whether of gold or silver, and get it made into whatever article he desires. There is a large quantity of native pottery in the form of flat dishes and bowls, with attractive colourings of brown, green and blue, and though the pottery is coarse a marvellous glaze is achieved nevertheless. The jars affixed to water-wheels are also of native work, and all turned on the potter's wheel:

> For in the Market-place, one Dusk of Day,
>> I watched the Potter thumping his wet Clay:
> And with its all-obliterated tongue
>> It murmured: 'Gently, Brother, gently, pray!

A certain amount of saddlery is made, and brass and copper utensils, but these are inferior to what is found in the bazaars of Bokhara.

Especially realizing the difficulty of bargaining without numerical help, I had to provide myself with the following table of figures, which does not show great extension of calculating powers on the part of the Khivans. The numbers are spelt phonetically:

bir	1	*igirma*	20
iki	2	*ottus*	30
outch	3	*quirk*	40
durt	4	*elley*	50
best	5	*olimish*	60
olta	6	*yettmish*	70
yetu	7	*secsem*	80
seccus	8	*toccsam*	90
toccus	9	*yus*	100
on	10	*eccus*	200
on bir	11	*mong*	1000
on iki	12		

After 100,000 the Russian numbers are used.

I spent one morning in visiting the new palace, as it is called in contradistinction to the old one, though it is by no means a modern building, and saw its garden and ponds, courts and verandas, the last supported on tall columns of carved wood, made from the Karagatch or black elm, one of the few timber trees of the country. The columns cost from one to five pounds apiece, and are a feature of all important residences.

I wished to see the harem, but 'purdah' is much more strictly enforced than in India, and no power of persuasion could admit me. The harem portion was guarded by a high mud wall, then being replaced by a brick one of native make. Flat squares are cemented in blocks of eight, and it is some comfort to find that building operations could be dilatory in Khiva as well as in Europe. One mason sat in front of a mud-hole, mixed clay with his hand, passed a handful of it to another, who gave an additional pat to it, and handed it on to another who laid it on the bricks. As the workmen were in occupation we were allowed to see the ladies' pleasure ground. In the centre there was a large stone basin of water on which floated tiny *caiouques*, or native boats, with baby oars; swings suspended from wooden bars with which to amuse themselves; benches and summer-houses in which to rest, with flower-beds of geraniums, petunias and roses to brighten up the scene; but how inadequate to brighten the dull lives that are spent there, as the women are never allowed out except in a Khivan cart whose arched top is completely covered over with rugs. Ten thousand roubles' worth of furniture had been ordered from Petrograd to furnish a new audience hall which was then being built.

The old palace is also worth seeing. Its design is of more interest. An entrance gate with towers at each side, not higher than twenty feet, is inlaid with bottle-green tiles, while along the façade is a row of loopholes. This is the most imposing part of the building, as the rest is like so many blank walls. The inner porch walls are covered with fine old turquoise-blue tiles of native design and workmanship, and the roof is supported by old carved Karagatch pillars. As the key of the palace had apparently been lost, we saw nothing further, but according to Colonel Korniloff there was nothing more to see. Captain Burnaby in 1876 thus described this palace:

> The Khan's palace is a large building ornamented with pillars and domes, which, covered with bright-coloured tiles, flash in the sun, and attract the attention of the stranger approaching Khiva. A guard of thirty or forty men armed with scimitars stood at the palace gates. The Khan's guards were all attired in long flowing silk robes of various patterns, bright-coloured sashes being girt around their waists, and tall fur hats surmounting their bronzed countenances. The

courtyard was surrounded by a low pile of buildings, which are the offices of the palace, and was filled with attendants and menials of the Court.

At the entrance to the palace is the prison, consisting of two cells, and at the time I saw it there were six prisoners in each. They were seated on the stone bench which runs round three sides of the room. Each man was fettered by the ankle to a long chain which passed underneath the door and was fastened to a peg in the ground outside. There was no light or air except from one small grated window and a hole in the roof, and through the gratings were passed the offerings of food made by the passers-by, as neither food nor work was given, and the prisoners were sometimes detained for days or even weeks.

These conditions have not changed since Captain Burnaby's day, as the following tells: –

We visited the prison – a low building on the left of the court which forms the entrance to the Khan's palace. Here I found two prisoners, their feet fastened in wooden stocks, whilst heavy iron chains encircled their necks and bodies.

The criminal law is rather a peculiar one, and with the utmost difficulty I managed to glean the following information. My mode of procedure was this: I spoke to my servant, Fritz, in German, and he had to find a native who spoke Russian. In the case of murder, the friends of the victim have the choice of demanding a fine or life for life. If sentenced to death, the sentence by hanging is carried out publicly; if fined, the prisoner is detained till it is paid. In the case of several convictions for theft, hanging is at last resorted to, and the Khan gives the sentence in all serious cases.

Manslaughter is also treated as murder, but if accidental a fine is imposed.

The Prime Minister kindly sent me an order to see the Summer Palace, by the hands of his dragoman, a fine-looking Turcoman, who arrived about one-thirty. He drank several tumblers of tea, then Colonel Korniloff and I set off with him, accompanied by two mounted outriders, who may have been added to do us honour, but unquestionably added to the dust (one of the afflictions of Khiva); still, thanks to their presence the traffic was cleared for us. The Summer Palace garden of several acres is surrounded by high walls of sun-dried clay and strengthened with buttresses, while an entrance is gained by wooden gates. It is laid out in Persian-like design, divided into small squares of about twenty feet by double rows of Lombardy poplars, between which flows a rivulet of water, and the squares are planted severally with quinces, pomegranates, figs, roses, cherries, plums, peaches and apricots, the whole effect giving somewhat the appearance of a chessboard. The figs and vines are laid flat in winter and covered with earth to protect them from the severe frosts.

There are groves of black elms, whose cobweb branches are extraordinarily beautiful in winter. This very characteristic deciduous tree, which is the chief timber-producing one of Turkestan, grows to a considerable size, though not to a great height. It is named the 'black elm,' from the peculiarly dark shade of its foliage. In the shade of those groves are erected open pavilions, in each of which is a throne for the Khan, so that in the burning hot days of summer he may laze away the hours reclining on luxurious cushions and costly rugs, listening to the cooling sound of dropping fountains. By one sat a melancholy pelican, looking for all the world like a deserted cat whom its owner had left behind. The palace is built in courts, with trees in the centre of each, the verandas of which were supported on tapering pillars, beautifully carved at the foot in not very deep relief, and unlike anything I had seen, though one might say a distinct Persian influence was visible.

The mosques next attracted attention, that of Palwanata being most worthy of note, from its large dome, surmounted by a golden ball, sixty feet high, and covered with very attractive old green tiles. This mosque, whose interior is lined with tiles in blue tracing Persian design, was founded by Palwanata, an early Khan, I was told, and attached to it is a school for teaching the blind to read, in order that they may employ themselves in the bazaars. Unhappily, blindness is very prevalent, owing to want of cleanliness in childhood, and the scourge of smallpox is also answerable for this most terrible of all afflictions.

The largest mosque and *medresse*, or college, were built by Madamin Khan in 1848, but unfortunately the tower was left unfinished owing to the death of the builder. In layers of light and dark blue and green and brown bricks, it has a striking appearance, and even though incomplete is a prominent architectural object in the town, from its height, which is not much short of a hundred and fifty feet. The students, about one hundred in number, are not limited as to time in their pursuit of knowledge, and some have been known to remain thirty and forty years! How characteristic this is of the East, where time means nothing in the divine search for knowledge, while we in the West in our universities often grudge the necessary three years' teaching. The following gives some idea of the course of studies pursued: –

Students are grouped, though not sharply, in three courses. In the lower course they are taught grammar and rhetoric; in the middle, dialectics and metaphysics; and in the upper,

ELLA R. CHRISTIE

jurisprudence, which also comprises the adoration of God.
The method of instruction is to commit to memory and
then receive comments thereon. A man who can say the
Koran from end to end, or, beginning at any part, can go on
repeating it, is deemed a scholar, though he may be utterly
unable to translate a chapter, and know nothing of Arabic.
Many study nothing but the Koran for eight or nine years.

The minarets of various mosques diversify a general view of
Khiva, the highest – that of Said Bai – being of a specially graceful
construction in burnt brick, with inlaid decoration of bottle-green
tiles.

The population of the town, which is about 20,000, like that of
all Central Asia, is a very mixed one, though Uzbegs predominate.
These are the descendants of Turkish tribes who migrated to
Central Asia before and after the time of Ginghiz Khan, and to
whom the Turcomans are supposed to be allied. They are divided
into something like ninety-two clans or families, who may, and
do, intermarry, but preserve their individuality in the male line.
The name Uzbeg means 'independent,' which is not unsuitable to
their present characteristics. The Sarts are universally the town-
dwellers, probably from choice, through having non-migratory
instincts, and yet they share a common origin with the Turcoman.

One also meets with Tajiks, who have more distinctive features,
being of Persian origin, while the familiar gipsies, or Liuli, which
is the name by which they are commonly known, ply their trade
of fortune-telling and petty commercial dealings, one of them
being almost a monopoly in the sale of leeches. I have seen Kirghiz,
but these I expect were only casual visitors on shopping errands,
and only temporarily absent from their tent homes. Their yellow
skins and flat Mongolian features are easily recognized in a crowd.

In winter the men wear fur-lined cloth bonnets tied under their chins with ear-flaps. The children of these various races are extraordinarily picturesque, usually dressed in red trousers and over-dress of red, with close-fitting mauve-coloured caps of brocade or Bokhara velvet ornamented with silver trinkets, and tufts of owl feathers are placed at one side to ward off the evil eye. This superstition of the evil eye is one of the few links which are common to both the East and the West.

The little girls are often adorned with a nose-ring or a jewelled button in their little nostrils: not exactly an improvement in our eyes, and they are in reality such pretty children, the chief characteristic which would strike a stranger being their beautiful complexions. It would be almost impossible to describe a group of them, so many and varied are the types – fair hair and blue eyes alongside of dark eyes and black hair, with all the intermediate shades of both. Having been duly schooled to avoid all appearance of the evil eye, a Kodak made them run like the wind when they caught sight of it.

Of domestic pets I was particularly attracted by the cats (and I am not a cat lover) – such lovely grey soft fur, something like the Persian breed but even softer in the coat.

The great amusement of men and boys is to tame a sparrow, and, tying a thread to its leg, let it perch on a finger and toss it off and on.

There are not many social distractions, but when a feast is given it is the custom to present all the sweets to the guest on leaving, and on one very important occasion Colonel Korniloff brought home about twenty pounds' weight of them. To each guest is also given a piece of sugar, and to the more important ones a small sugar loaf. No sugar is sold already broken, but only in sugar loaves, and so a necessary article in every house is a pair of sugar pincers. Sugar is not always put in tea, but a small piece is bitten off and the tea sucked through it, as being a more economical mode of using it. The sign of betrothal is said 'to have given sugar.'

There appear to be no taxes except 2½ per cent, on rents, which is paid to the Khan. The roads are as nature made them, and therefore no upkeep is required. All through the town are irrigation canals, which have every year to be cleared and banks maintained, which is done by the cultivators of the soil. They also give a water supply to those houses unprovided with wells.

The Khanate of Khiva has an area about double that of Great Britain and has a population of from 800,000 to 900,000 inhabitants. The other towns of importance are Novi Urgentsch, Hasarasp, Kuni Urgentsch and Petro Alexandrovsk, the military centre. Hasarasp is supposed to be identical with Zariaspe, to which place Alexander the Great retired his troops for the winter from Samarkand, and there is rather a charming legend respecting it.

'Popular tradition,' says M. Kuhn, 'records that in olden time there lived four kings – two of them infidels and two Mussulmans, one of the latter being Iskander Suleiman. Suleiman conquered all the world, tamed every living thing, and subjected to his rule even the inhabitants of the spirit world. On one occasion Suleiman ascended his throne, which by the spirits was lifted in the air, so that he might inspect the entire earth; and then he alighted where now stands Hasarasp. At that period the locality was covered with beautiful meadows and dense forests, through which ran a stream of sparkling water. At the moment of Suleiman's descent a thousand graceful steeds had come to drink. The king ordered his attendant spirits to catch the horses, and when they could not do so, he directed an intoxicating liquor to be put in the stream, which enabled the spirits to fulfil his command, ever since which time the horse has been in subjection to man. Having possessed himself of the steeds, Suleiman caused a fortress to be erected on the spot, and called it "Hazarasp," or a thousand horses.'

Farm-houses are scattered around, and are protected from marauders by a high surrounding mud wall. Inside is the dwelling-house and space for fodder, with a look-out tower exactly such as one finds on the Indian frontier at the present day, and probably similar to those which existed in the castles of Scotland hundreds of years ago. The houses are built of sun-dried brick, and for the foundation a layer of mud is first spread, then a layer of branches, which is next thickly filled up with reeds among the mud bricks. In order to give greater strength the walls slope inwards, and are further strengthened by posts and supporting buttresses; the whole is then plastered over with mud, both inside and out, and while still wet patterns are impressed on the outside, chiefly of a fluted design. The roofing consists of reeds laid on fairly substantial sticks, and where there is a veranda it is covered with reed mats. The entrance door to the court is a very substantial one, studded at top and bottom with heavy brass bosses, and closed by a massive wooden beam and bolts. This fashion of building applies also to the houses in towns, so that as one stands at the end of a street of dwelling-houses the effect is a most curious one, for the walls are absolutely without windows, the only exception being an occasional slit, and this is again emphasized by the doors occurring at long intervals. They are barred at nightfall, and admittance is gained only by a needle's eye, all recalling troublous times when life was perilously uncertain, and the danger of incursion by nomadic hordes might mean death and unspeakable horrors. One of the most picturesque touches is the large green glazed water-jars to be found in most courtyards, and the form is possibly a reminiscence of the Greek occupation.

There are two distinct species of sheep to be found, the most numerous being the fat-tailed variety, whose tail provides the animal with sustenance in the same way as does the camel's hump, and it is also the substitute for the oil and butter of other countries.

From the other species is obtained the lambskin known as caracul in the fur trade, which provides the headgear in universal use among the inhabitants of Turkestan, not only in white, but in black, grey and brown. The other domestic animals are cattle, camels, horses, donkeys and goats. Mutton is the meat most commonly used, and the wool of the sheep is spun and woven by hand and then made into the long coats worn by all, while the coarser hair serves to make felt rugs. Cattle are used in ploughing and as beasts of burden; the old wooden plough has not been superseded, as the modern iron one was tried but found unsuitable for the land. Native harrows consist of a wooden beam, beneath which is fixed a double row of wooden pegs, and the necessary weight is attained by the driver standing on the beam while being dragged in jerks across the roughest ground. Such powers of balance can only be acquired through heredity.

Corn, maize, rice and a species of vetch used for fodder are grown, and lucerne is exported to the value of three to four million roubles. Cotton, too, is taking an important place, and the latest figures I had showed that the total amount per annum had reached a figure of one million poods (a pood is equal to about forty pounds avoirdupois). The seed is made into oil and oil-cake, and a strange form of the latter is that of jars in which the oil is stored. Liquorice, too, is an export.

Melons of many varieties are found, and grapes are also grown, though when grown in the open the vines have to be buried in winter owing to the severe frosts. Farming is carried on chiefly by the Uzbegs, as the wealth of the Kirghiz consists in flocks and herds, which render them a nomadic people, or, being nomadic, they have confined their attention to that branch of farming.

According to Dr Schuyler in his interesting book on Central Asia:

'The Kirghiz, owing to the simplicity of their lives, are far more children of nature than other Asiatics, and have all the faults and virtues of children. Probably the first acquaintance with them will be found disagreeable, and certainly the side the casual traveller sees is their worst, but upon knowing them more intimately, one cannot help liking and even respecting them, and it is the verdict of everyone who has lived in Central Asia that the Kirghiz are superior to all the other races.'

Their features are not unpleasing, and very often in the older people there is a benevolent expression, which in the case of the women can be seen, as they are neither veiled nor secluded. In cold weather the men's heads are enveloped in fur-lined caps with ear-flaps. The Sarts are the town-dwellers and shopkeepers, and this applies all over Russian Central Asia. They are honest in so far as when a bargain has been made they will stick to it, and in all the months I spent in the country, and constantly in crowds, I never had an article stolen or pocket picked. But then perhaps I had nothing worth stealing.

IX

Battle, Murder & Sudden Death

Russian Ambition – Conquest of Khiva –
Brutalities Practised – A Fated Expedition – An
Enlightened Minister – Assassination

The known history of the Khanate of Khiva is of an extremely fragmentary character. Originally it formed part of the conquests of Alexander the Great in 334 B.C., and it was then merged into the Bactrian kingdoms, followed by Parthian, Persian, and then Arab rule. In 1092 it became an independent state, and we presume that it was sufficiently prosperous to attract the devastating hordes of Ginghiz Khan in 1221, when its capital, Novi Urgentsch, was destroyed, and Khiva was then made the chief town of the Khanate. The next avalanche that descended on the country was the expedition of Timur, or Tamerlane, in 1379, and for a considerable time it was ruled by his descendants, until the people revolted against them and elected as Khan in 1512 Sultan Ilbars of the Uzbeg dynasty. The Uzbegs are descendants of Turkish tribes who at different periods have migrated to Central Asia. The present ruler is of that lineage. Various attempts were made by the Russians ever since they entered Central Asia to subdue the country, on the plea that the Khivans encourage rebellion among the Kirghiz, a nomadic people inhabiting Turkestan, and claiming descent from one of the nine sons of Noah, who is said to have settled in Turkestan on the banks of the Amu Daria, and was the father of forty daughters. In reality they are a Turkish race and speak the dialect of the Uzbegs.

As early as 1620 there were diplomatic relations with Russia, and about that date some Cossacks of the Ural, hearing of the wealth of Khiva, were able actually to reach the town of Novi Urgentsch, which they plundered, carrying off much booty and nearly one thousand women. The Khivans intercepted their flight and cut them off from water, slaughtering them almost to a man. A second and third Cossack expedition met with no better success, nature's desert barrier forming Khiva's surest protection. A rumour of the golden sands of the Amu Daria having reached Peter the Great, his cupidity led him to fit out two expeditions in 1717, one from Siberia into little Bokhara, and the other to Khiva under Prince Bekovitch. According to an account given by Schuyler:

'Prince Bekovitch occupied three years with surveys of the eastern shore of the Caspian and the establishment of various fortified positions, and it was not until June 1717 that he moved over the Steppe towards Khiva with an army of 3500 men, 6 guns, and a train of 200 camels and 300 horses. When about one hundred miles from that city, on the banks of the Amu Daria, he had a decisive battle with the Khivans, which lasted three days and ended in the complete defeat of the latter. The Khan surrendered himself unreservedly to the mercy of the Russians, and after obtaining the full confidence of Prince Bekovitch, proposed to him to go and take actual possession of Khiva, after dividing his army into several parts for the greater convenience of provisioning it. This was no sooner done than the Khivans treacherously fell upon the separate portions of the expedition, massacred them almost without exception, and sent the head of Prince Bekovitch as a present to the Emir of Bokhara, who, however, refused to accept it.'

Various pacific attempts were afterwards made, especially by an Italian, Florio Benevelli, an envoy of Peter the Great, to induce the Khan to come to terms and to cease capturing and enslaving Russians, but with no success. Tales are still extant of the brutalities perpetrated on the unfortunate captives. Men were shod with iron and Russian women filled the harems. These disorders induced General Perovsky in 1829 to fit out another punitive expedition, consisting of 5000 men, 22 guns, 10,000 camels and 2000 Kirghiz to take care of them. By a strange lack of foresight they started in late autumn. Winter began earlier and was more severe than usual. Transports were lost in the blinding snowstorms, and before they reached half-way the retreat was ordered; and a tragic one it was; only one-third of the men survived in a more or less dying condition, and only a thousand camels struggled back. After warning had been given of another expedition contemplated by the Russians, the summer of 1840 saw the Khivans in a more reasonable frame of mind, and they returned 418 Russian captives, with the promise that no more Russians were to be made slaves.

In 1842 another envoy was sent, and induced the Khan to sign a treaty 'not to engage in hostilities against Russia, or to commit acts of robbery and piracy.' This the Khan regarded as a 'scrap of paper,' and when in 1858, on the outbreak of fresh troubles, Colonel Ignatief reminded him of this document he was told that it could not be found in the archives, and no one believed it had ever existed. Further arguments were useless, and in 1869 and 1870 the Khivans, whether rightly or wrongly, were again accused of inciting the Kirghiz to rebellion. This is apparently denied by General Tchernaief in the following speech: –

'The Khivans did not excite the Kirghiz to rebellion; on the contrary, they were made to rebel by the introduction of the new regulations composed under the supervision of the Ministry of War, the liberal and humane aims of which somehow always meet a strange fate. So it was in the present instance. Instead of the expected gratitude of the population for the introduction of the humane and liberal regulations the only reply was rebellion. When Cossack detachments were sent out to put down these disturbances, the Kirghiz threw the blame on the distant Khivans, and the officials accepted these excuses to cover their own mistakes. In this way the idea grew up at St Petersburg of the instigation of the Kirghiz by the Khivans, who had no thought for foreign undertakings when they could scarcely maintain themselves at home against the Turcomans.'

Whatever be the cause, the Russians felt that the situation from their point of view was unsatisfactory, so in 1873 three expeditions were fitted out to start from Tashkent, Orenburg and Krasnovodsk, distant respectively 600, 930 and 500 miles, all three to be under the command of General Kauffmann, who wished to reserve for himself the honour of capturing Khiva. It was a disastrous path that led to it. In the desert of Kara-Kum his force nearly perished from want of water and food. The biscuits which had been sent with the expedition had been stored for years at Tashkent, the chief town of Russian Central Asia, and were worm-eaten and mouldy. It was impossible to advance or to retreat, from lack of transport. General Kauffmann was on the brink of despair when a ray of hope appeared in the shape of a wandering Kirghiz, who indicated that they were within a few miles of the wells of Alty-Kuduk. General Kauffmann handed him his pocket flask and offered him one hundred roubles reward if he would bring it back filled with water. This was speedily done, and men and animals were sent on to the wells, which were few in number, but sufficed to save the remnant of men and beasts. Of the 10,000 camels that started but 1200 remained. The whole distance from Khalata was strewn with camp equipment and munitions of war, while decaying bodies of camels and horses filled the air with a stench that was intolerable.

Meantime General Kauffmann pursued his way to Khiva and received the peaceable submission of the city, and then occupied the Khan's palace. All reasonable precautions were taken to preserve the property and safety of the harem, the inmates of which had remained, while orders were given to disarm the inhabitants, at the same time assuring them of the clemency of the Tsar, and that all he desired was that they should live peaceably and pursue their ordinary avocations. The soldiers were strictly forbidden to take anything from the inhabitants, and to pay cash for whatever was required. Slavery was abolished, and those who were Persians had the option of remaining or returning to their native country. It is sad to have to record how these humane and civilized proceedings were marred. A levy of 300,000 roubles was laid upon the Turcoman inhabitants of the Khanate, which had to be paid within ten days. Their wealth, consisting solely of flocks and herds, made it impossible to realize this tremendous sum of money on such short notice, and an order was therefore issued by General Kauffmann 'to give over the settlements of the Yomuds and their families to complete destruction, and their herds and property to confiscation.'

The report of an eye-witness testifies to the manner in which this order was carried out:

'When we had gone about twenty-five miles from Khiva, General Golovatchy said before a large number of officers in my presence: "I have received an order from the Commander-in-Chief. I hope you will remember it and give it to your soldiers. This expedition does not spare either sex or age. Kill all of them." After this the officers delivered this command to their several detachments, and that it was carried out the following will show: "We burned as we had done before – grain, houses and everything which we met, and the cavalry, which was in advance, cut down every person, man, woman, or child.' "

One is glad to believe that General Golovatchy was personally not to blame for this appalling butchery, but was merely carrying out the *imperial* orders.

The total cost of the expedition came to about four million pounds sterling, and would have been still more had the Kirghiz been paid for their camels. The Prefect of Perovsky told them that as they never would be paid they had better make a present of them to the Russians, and they actually signed an address to General Kauffmann to that effect, while he in return received one from the Tsar 'thanking the inhabitants of the province of Turkestan for their noble conduct, and their loyalty expressed by such a great sacrifice.'

Before the troops finally left, they began the construction of the fort, Petro Alexandrovsk, which is now the chief military depot in Central Asia. It was difficult to get the exact numbers of troops, but I gathered they might be approximately thirty thousand.

Since then Khiva has had a form of self-government under a Khan. 'The Khanate descends from father to son, and not to the eldest male relative, as is the case amidst some other Mahommedan nations. The monarch receives the Crown lands and gardens intact. With the rest of the nation, the property at a father's death is divided equally amongst his sons, thus doing away with the possibility of anyone possessing a larger extent of the soil. The actual Khan, after paying his annual tribute to the Tsar, has 100,000 roubles, or about 14,000 pounds, a year left for himself. He has no army to maintain.' There is a resident Russian Commissioner ostensibly in the Khan's service, who helps to guide native rule and supervise the payment of an annual tribute. Colonel Korniloff occupied that position for over twenty years, when he and his wife were barbarously murdered by the Bolshevists on the outbreak of the Russian revolution. During the time of my visit in 1912 Islam Hodja acted as chief minister to the Khan, a most enlightened man, 'the only native with whom I could have intelligent dealings,' as Colonel Korniloff described him, and therefore to him it must have been a special loss when a few months after my return home I received from Madame Korniloff the following sad news: –

Dans notre ville il se produisait un incident effroyable: le grand vizir Seid-Islam-Chodja mourut des mains des scélé-rats. L'affaire se passa le 4 Août à 4 heures du soir. Islam Chodja sortit accompagné d'autres ministères du palais du chan et se rendit en voiture à la maison. Son cocher était avec lui. Près d'un cimetière tout couvert de hauts roseaux les conspirateurs se jetèrent sur le voiture et arrêtèrent le cheval. Ils donnerent au cocher quelques coups du sabre à son bras gauche. Le cocher s'enfuit. Islam Chodja prit la fuite aussi, mais n'ayant fait que dix pas de la voiture il fut saisi et tué par les assassins. Aux cris du cocher blessé les gardes se rassemblèrent, mais les conspirateurs eurent temps de se cacher. Informé de cet incident mon mari se rendit sur la place de l'assassinat. Islam Chodja était couché au milieu de la rue dans une mer de sang. Sur la tête il avait quatre blessures sabrées, son cou etait coupé. C'est son fils Abdoul Saliam qui fut destiné à sa place. Les assassins ne sont pas retrouvés. Tout le monde regrette Islam Chodja comme un homme sage et bon qui faisait beaucoup de bien à son pays.

Ne nous oubliez pas et venez chez nous. Votre

Natalie Korniloff

Translation of the Letter from Madame Korniloff

A terrible event has occurred in our town. The Grand Vizier has died at the hands of ruffians. The event took place on 4th August at four P.M. Islam Hodja had left the Khan's palace accompanied by other ministers and had started to drive home. His coachman was with him. Near a cemetery completely concealed by tall willows the conspirators threw themselves on the carriage and stopped the horse. They slashed the coachman's left arm several times with a sword. The coachman fled. Islam Hodja tried also to escape, but when only ten paces from the carriage he was seized and killed by the murderers. The cries of the wounded coachman brought out the guard, but the scoundrels had time to hide. Hearing of what had happened, my husband rushed to the scene of the murder. Islam Hodja was lying in the street in a pool of blood with four sword wounds on his head and his throat cut. His son Abdul Saliam was the intended victim. The assassins have not yet been found. Everyone mourns Islam Hodja as being a great and good man who did much for the good of his country.

Do not forget us and return to us. Your
NATALIE KORNILOFF.

Such are the tragedies that seem to pursue life in Khiva.

X

Khiva to Petro Alexandrovsk

A Beg's Hospitality – A Cart Journey – A Lengthy Send-off – Embarkation – A Crowded Cabin – Family Prayers

After taking leave of my kind hosts I started in the early morning on my desert journey to Petro Alexandrovsk, thanks to the kindness of Islam Hodja, who, not unmindful of his promise to drive me there, sent his carriage, a hooded one, with his own horse and one which he had borrowed from his brother; consequently they were not accustomed to run in a pair. We escaped ditches and bazaar shops in a hair-raising manner, and when half-way to a finish the galloper got its hind leg over the shaft. I was out in a trice. Fritz was most useful and quickly refitted the harness, but not before both horses had sat down on their hind legs like circus performers, though luckily neither dreamt of kicking. The track led across a desert of sand and salt, varied by an occasional oasis. At forty versts from Khiva we reached Hanki, where the Beg had orders to receive me. He had a fine house with courtyards, whose supporting pillars were elaborately carved and mounted on limestone pedestals. His son was waiting on the veranda to offer a welcome. I ascended some steps and shook hands on dismounting from my queer shay, and he then led me through two saloons furnished in European style. In the second saloon was a table on which was set out the *dasturkan* with six dishes of sweets, of Russian and native manufacture, in poisonous colours of blue and yellow. Two large scones were placed on the table in front of each chair, which were of European make. Tea was ordered and, after breakfast at five A.M., was not unwelcome at eleven; neither were the sweets, and even half of one of my scones, though I had a secret feeling it was really meant as a plate; when not observed, I rolled the other half in my 'hanky' for future use, thinking we should get no more food.

To my surprise we were summoned to the next room, and by this time a good-looking man appeared, speaking Russian, whom I took to be the Beg; he bade me be seated, and then in came the real Beg, the chief one for Khiva district, for whom all rose to their feet – an equally fine-looking man, with a particularly good type of face. He also welcomed me, and we then partook of an excellent meat stew washed down by mineral water, and our scones were brought in from the next room, mine, alas, lacking. I then asked if I might photograph the family, which greatly pleased its male members, the females being never seen. The Beg went and put on all his medals and orders, as well as two really beautifully mounted gold-handled swords, one set with turquoises and the other with rubies and emeralds, doubtless presentations from the Tsar. We were next bidden again to drink tea, while the Beg disappeared, and returning presented me with three gold coins, two over five hundred years old, found at Kuni Urgentsch, and the third old Khivan; all three fine specimens. He told me he had been notified three months ago by the Russian officials, who during this journey showed me every consideration, that an English lady was coming to Hanki, and all help was to be given her and whatever horses she required, so accordingly he sent me off in his own carriage to the river, a distance of five versts, his brother riding as escort. A *caiouque* was commandeered at the riverside, and for two and a half hours, with a fair wind blowing, we sailed along with the help of the large square sail in use on the Amu Daria, while the native passengers lent their aid in managing it. The Beg sent his coachman with us all the way to save any trouble. I distributed raisins among the passengers, who ate them as curiosities coming from London, and led them to believe our climate is better than it is generally given credit for.

On arriving at the landing stage for Petro Alexandrovsk we had still four or five versts to go before reaching the town, and these had to be done in an *arba,* a high-wheeled native cart that also carried the luggage. With the help of a sack of corn I was able to mount, and the cart drive was not so uncomfortable as I had expected, though these giant wheels throw up so much dust.

Petro Alexandrovsk was reached by evening, and the Korniloffs having given me the key of their house there, I installed my bed in what was a three-roomed cottage, somewhat sparsely furnished, with the arrangement that feeding was to be done at the *Cloob*, as there is no inn in this military station of several thousand men, Cossacks and artillery.

Captain and Mrs Muchaloff, the Korniloff son-in-law and his wife, had quite a comfortable house, very unlike the ordinary residence of Russians of their class. I called on Madame Licoshin, the wife of the Commandant of the district, with whom I travelled on the steamer. He was away on tour, and she was living in one small room at the *Cloob*; in one corner was a bed for herself, and in another one for the maid. All the cooking was done in the same room, and platters of cooked and uncooked food were scattered about. Apparently, however, she was quite content with this simple *ménage*, though marvelling at my travelling in *caiouques* and carts.

There are a number of native shops, which are all shut except twice a week, when they open for business on market days. There is one Russian store with a miscellaneous assortment of goods for sale; also a bakery, producing the worst bread I have ever tasted; as it was very uncertain when it could be had at all most housekeepers baked their own bread. Samarkand, a station on the railway, four days' journey from the Russian border, is looked upon by the Russians as the height of bliss; one lady sighed as she thought of its delights and proximity to Moscow. Of course Petro Alexandrovsk is rather banishment, as no boat sails at all from November to the beginning of March, and the only communication with Charjui is by riding, or camel *telega*, along a route where there are no rest-houses worthy of the name. But in these towns one could not help being struck with the great lack of rational amusement among the military. In similar circumstances our men would have had polo, big-game shooting, tennis, and the usual diversions of an Indian station; but here, wherever one went, there was nothing but drinking and gambling.

To celebrate the departure of the Commandant a merry party assembled to lunch at the *Cloob* one day at twelve o'clock. Happening on the following morning to visit the scene of revelry, at the same hour, I found the dining-room bestrewn with cigarette ends and matches, and the green cloth of the card-table crossed and recrossed with chalked-up figures. It appeared on inquiry that the party had broken up only an hour before, having sat up all night drinking and gambling! Surely a lengthy send-off!

Rumours of the boat having arrived caused wild excitement, and hearing of the large number of would-be passengers, I started at six A.M. with my luggage and Fritz in an *arba*, in the delightful uncertainty of how and where we were to reach the ship: for however much one asks, no one really knows. After jolting for an hour we reached the river, but by no means in sight of our steamer. A *caiouque* was waiting, into which we transferred ourselves and luggage, and presently were joined by a 'commercial' whom we knew. By many bendings and turnings of the stream we were towed, and were finally dropped on the shore of an island which had to be crossed in an *arba*. Then came the welcome sight of a funnel, and no Crusoe ever looked more eagerly for a sail than I did! The captain could give me a berth only in one of the two second-class cabins, as all the first were required for the retiring Commandant, and Buchaloff and his three sons, on their way to Moscow for the opening of the Alexander III. memorial. Very fine they looked in brand-new silk *khalats* bought for the occasion, rustling with stiffness and gloss, which is achieved by a lump of glass inserted at the end of a hanging pole being passed rapidly backwards and forwards on the silk as it is spread on a hard board. His friend the Beg of Hanki came in a gorgeous green silk *khalat*, with one of his fine dirks in his sash-band, to see him off.

A *shamiana*, or coloured tent, was erected on the bleak shore in which the General and notabilities, including Buchaloff, lunched, and in honour, I suppose, of his temperance principles bottles of very frothy pink liquid were served. One can never forget the picturesque groups that camped in the open while waiting for the departure. That was the last bright spot.

To be shut up for six days in a second-class cabin, the size of a decent four-berth one, with five women and six children, one a babe, is equally memorable; no proper berths, merely a shelf on which were already many occupants, so that *aragatz* had to be plentifully sprinkled. I secured a port-hole and thus avoided suffocation, but as my companions, who numbered eleven to one, were terrified of air, I could only open this surreptitiously during the night. It was impossible to sleep, as the baby cried invariably as soon as one had dropped off. The feeding of those children was amazing, the day beginning with sardines, a thickly iced and jammed cake, and cheese. At dinner I saw a child of certainly not more than two years of age eat a plate of *bortsch,* not such as we know it, but a greasy mixture of half-cooked cubes of turnips and sour cabbage, adding thereto chicken and underdone cabinet pudding, and between whiles seizing large morsels of pickled gherkins. By six P.M. my cabin companions were tearing dried fish in pieces (this bundle of fish was part of their cabin luggage), and devouring them with bread and cheese, to the accompaniment of tea, and by seven-thirty P.M. were consuming another enormous meal in the saloon. Even the gherkin baby was having meat and *compote.* The result was as follows, with apologies to Addison: –

> Soon as the evening shades prevail,
> The babe takes up its doleful wail,
> And nightly to the crowd below
> In cries and screams proclaims its woe!

One night it nearly yelled itself into convulsions, and went on for half-an-hour, its relatives seeming to heed it no more than they did the feelings of the passengers.

The General's household goods, in the form of chairs, tables and plants, were all piled on the paddle-box, with not even a cover over them. Every inch of deck space was filled with natives and their bundles, the sailors good-naturedly working under those trying conditions and never complaining. We tied up as usual each night, and when Buchaloff went ashore his servants spread rugs, his own rather in front of the others, when he led his suite in family worship. Behind the kneeling row a hole had been dug and a fire lighted, by which stood his *chilim,* his spouted water-pot, and native samovar, to supply his creature comforts as soon as prayers were finished. After the customary invocations he appeared to add some personal requests, and then refastening his sash-belt around his waist, and replacing his slippers, he knelt upon his rug, and the *chilim* was then handed to him, together with a teapot and handleless cup. Scattered groups on shore were clearly seen in the starry night, and on deck beneath the electric light was a little trio representative of the means that made such a sight possible – the Russian General, the banker, and the captain – while borne aloft were the strains of the soldiers' evening hymn.

XI

Bokhara the Noble

*A Central Asia Tip – Rough Quarters – A
Walled-in Town – Hindoos – A Sart Home –
Street Watering – Crowded Lanes – Rugs*

The hues of youth upon a brow of woe,
Which men called old two thousand years ago:
Match me such marvel save in Eastern clime,
A rose-red city – half as old as time.

Sandbanks not providing more than the usual delays, Charjui was once more reached at the end of six days' journey from Petro Alexandrovsk. A welcome relief from the cramped conditions on board was the Hotel Nazarro, which was small but clean and comfortable; and what would not have been luxury after my week's experience on board the Oxus steamer? It was kept by the wife of the boat steward, who shared her meals with the hotel guests.

My window looked into a garden of white mulberries and fast-ripening cherries, for it was then the 19th of May, while it also offered a sample of the usual Russian extremes. Seeing something glistening between the bushes, I went out to explore, and suddenly realized that it was a piece of lovely old brocade with gold-thread design, being used for a chicken shelter!

I also had the enlivenment of the bleating of a black lamb beneath my window, and on asking the reason of its presence there, was told that it was given by Buchaloff to the steward of the boat. Doubtless this was the Central Asia manner of a grandee's tip! I suppose he had provided it for his own eating on the journey, and this not being unduly prolonged, there were not sufficient dishes of *pilau* required to use it up; further, it would have been an inconvenient bit of luggage to lead to Moscow.

Farewells had at length to be said to the garden of green parakeets and blue-birds and nightingales, and I made an early start one morning for Bokhara, a wearisome journey of one hundred and forty-one miles eastwards.

The railway crosses sandy deserts whose depressions are filled by salt deposits, the surface broken here and there by plants of camel thorn, stunted tamarisk, or *saxaul*. Occasional mounds revealed some buried city, deserted because of the failure of water.

Nearing Bokhara the scene changes to one of brilliant verdure in spring, as the city is surrounded by trees and gardens watered by rippling streams. Kagan, the junction for Bokhara, which was reached late at night, offers few attractions – a miry swamp in wet weather, and little vegetation to clothe the rather bleak appearance which it presents. Only one droshky, or Russian carriage, and this had been already appropriated, was in waiting at the station, but by dint of a bribe to the driver he returned, and for an hour and a half we drove through morasses of stiff mud, narrowly avoiding in the darkness many a mud-hole, to find the two European hotels and three native ones full to overflowing. Not one human being more could be accommodated in the somewhat restricted limits of those one-storey inns. The situation seemed rather desperate from my point of view as to where the rest of the night was to be passed. The station seemed the most hopeful place to try, as it might possibly offer a covered truck. Accordingly I roused the station-master, and after much parleying he allowed me to establish my bed in the none too clean waiting-room. As a matter of precaution I surrounded it on the floor with a ring of *Aragatz* powder, guaranteed to allow no insect to cross its Brünhilde-like barrier.

Sleep was impossible after six A.M. owing to the noisy crowds that began to collect, so I decided to take the first train for Bokhara, some twelve miles off. The Russians in all their settling of the country never failed to observe the rule of leaving the native city to itself, its own laws and customs, and building a European town on their own lines more or less distant from the other. From the moment of arrival on the platform there was a series of enchanting pictures, and by evening I felt as if I had been witnessing some wonderful pageant.

Bokhara is completely walled round by a twenty-eight-feet high wall, seven and a half miles in circuit, with eleven gates, all rigidly closed at eight P.M., when the watchmen set out on their rounds beating a drum to show that they are awake, which must be such a useful warning for would-be robbers. Having secured a room at a caravanserai kept by an Armenian, I moved in my baggage; my portable bed and suit-cases were the furnishing, for nothing was provided but the empty room. Had I ridden there on a camel or donkey, they would have been stabled in the court below. When evening fell the whole establishment was closed in by a huge nail-studded door, strongly barred, with a mouse-hole of an entrance at one side and a peep-hole through which to inspect the would-be entrant, all telling of troublous times. The only window my room was possessed of looked on to the court-yard, but through its open sash, when night fell, came the low musical whistle of the blind masseurs reminding tired and aching

limbs that there was a remedy at hand, for massage is much practised in Bokhara.

As to the question of food, the traveller has to make his own
arrangements. Nothing is obtainable in the inn unless it be the
standard bowl of *pilau* cooked once a day. Restaurants, or their
equivalent, are wayside stalls offering bits of mutton broiled on
skewers, and certain kinds of fried foods which emit a savoury
smell; while drinks are to be had from the sherbet-seller who
clinks his brass bowls as he walks along the street, or from the
numerous tea-houses which serve as a form of club to the natives.
Green tea is usually preferred, though the Indian merchants are
pushing their own line of trade.

The luxurious food of the rich is thus picturesquely described
by Matthew Arnold:

> In vain therefore with wistful eyes
> Gazing up hither, the poor man,
> Who loiters by the high-heaped booths,
> Below, there in the Registan
> Says, 'Happy he who lodges there!
> With silken raiment, store of rice,
> And for this drought all kinds of fruits,
> Grape syrup, squares of coloured ice.

The population was said to be about 70,000 to 100,000, doubtless considerably diminished since the Bolshevik regime with its
wholesale slaughtering. The Sarts are the town-dwellers and
traders, but mixed with them are various races. Tajiks and Turcomans, Uzbegs and Kirghiz are all to be met with, as well as a
considerable Jewish population. Settled there for countless generations, these last still have to suffer for the sins of their fathers, and

wear a distinctive dress, which includes a cloth cap limited as to fur trimming, and a string girdle. The young Jewesses are exceedingly beautiful, though they age early, and the children with their amazing complexions are indeed fair to look upon. The tea trade is carried on by a colony of Indian Moslems of the strict sect of Sunnites. One, a Peshawari, was presented to me as he spoke English. He said his religion forbade him talking to a woman, but he would do so through a third party. Conversation was thus somewhat difficult to maintain, more especially as he spoke excellent English. The final question finished me: 'Does she travel and what is the future disposition of her plans?'

The 'future disposition' of my plans led me off after this to further exploration in the bazaars. These are indeed a dream, with their motley crowds, the wealthier members in gorgeous-coloured *khalats* in silk, velvet, or cloth of gold, while the less opulent wear Bokhara cottons in rainbow colourings: of which I always feel sure Joseph's coat of many colours must have been made, as these cottons, silks and velvets have been famed for centuries. A few of the populace had, I regret to say, preferred Manchester flowered cretonnes, making their figures look like perambulating furniture. On their shaven heads turbans, more or less large according to the means and social standing of the wearer, were worn by all, wound round a coloured or stitched skull-cap, called a *tepey tate* (phonetically spelt) with an end of the turban hanging down at one side. A woman is hardly ever seen on the street; if she is ever met with, she is enveloped in a huge grey cloak, a square of horsehair covering her face. By invitation one day I visited a Sart's house in order to see his home, as he was accounted a man with advanced views and a large fortune. At the entrance a cow and calf were tethered in what one might call the entrance hall. Next was a court with reception-rooms in European style and Bokhara decoration – that is to say, the walls were lined with gaily painted carved niches, which serve instead of drawers or cabinets; the floors were laid with costly native rugs and carpets, so shoes had to be removed before stepping on them. I was then led on to the women's quarter by a little son of the house, who showed it off with the airs of a *père de famille*, and with great dignity, in his little flowered coat and turban.

Two young wives, fair in complexion, and two old women were the occupants, dressed in Bokhara red and yellow silk trousers, over which was a sort of coloured chemise in silk or muslin, and a profusion of jewellery, among which coral seemed greatly in favour, judging from the many strings of bright red beads around their necks. Their hair was dressed in countless little plaits ending in handsome ornamental and jewelled tassels. On their heads were little silk caps, round the edge of which was tied a high stiff hand-kerchief. Various children were running about, and even the little girls had two nose-rings apiece, one a button and one a pendent one. So uncomfortable they must be, but pride – even in Bokhara – feels no pain. An infant in its cradle in the corner of the room was so covered up in silk wrappings that I wondered it was not smothered, and one woman explained, it was a 'Niña.'

There was no sign of anything to occupy their time except a sewing machine, and they were all crunching sunflower seeds out of their henna-dyed fingers as they sat cross-legged on the rug-covered floor. One chair was carried from room to room for my benefit by one of the little girls, who finally tumbled over it, much to the amusement of the others. We all shook hands at parting (as do the shopkeepers when a bargain is struck), and one could not help feeling that there is something lacking in the religion of Mahomet that can condemn women to such a life as is led even in the house of an enlightened Sart.

The bazaars of Bokhara for centuries have been famed throughout the world. To the uninitiated this represents the trading quarters of the town, in which are situated the shops. The streets of the more important ones are arched over and lighted by circular openings in the roof. Miles of tortuous lanes have a covering of poplar or willow sticks, upon which are laid sods of turf, or reeds, or matting – anything to keep out the fierce glare of sunlight, and by those means they are kept delightfully cool. To allay the dust, the primitive method is adopted of a man carrying on his back a skin filled with water, from the neck of which he skilfully manipulates the desired spray.

Carts, carriages and animals of all kinds jostle along to the cries of '*pusht, pusht,*' which means 'take care': a necessary warning, as the only refuge for foot-passengers is a raised step which is laid along the front of the open shops. Upon this one can sit and bargain comfortably until perhaps a heavily laden Bactrian camel comes along, threatening to sweep off everything before it. Then a block occurs, as unregulated traffic pours in from side alleys, and the high-wheeled carts get interlocked and strident voices are upraised, and no one will move, as each one seems determined to maintain every inch of ground gained, and time is no object. Paving of any kind is unknown, so in wet weather, with greasy mud to negotiate, there is much difficulty before all obstructions are removed.

The various trades have their own localities, all of which lends itself to the universal system of bargaining, without which nothing can be bought or sold. If a deal cannot be effected with one, another is ready and at hand, and I never failed to find intense interest taken by the lookers-on, not to speak of help proffered on more than one occasion, and quite impartially: a friend of the seller would implore him not to lose such a chance, and if I walked away further chaffering would be continued between the two on their own account, till a reasonable figure was reached and hands were shaken by all concerned in the purchase. The Russian coinage was the recognized one, but various misshapen bits of brass and copper used to change hands. The only native coin of value was the *tilla*, a small gold coin then worth about thirteen shillings.

For colouring, the saddlery bazaar ranked high. The wooden saddles, with their high pommel in front, painted in a species of lacquer, whose glorious reds shone amid the work of the various inlaid designs, were specially attractive. The horse trappings, sufficient to deck a horse from nose to tail, were of leather, covered with metal ornaments of brass, and even of silver, with coloured bosses, beads and feathers; nothing omitted that could make a pony as gay as a macaw.

Not far off from the saddlery bazaar is that of the shoe and boot makers. The shopkeeper in his coloured robe and stitched skull-cap kneels in the centre of his open-fronted shop, while behind him the wall is hung with pairs of soft leather boots in the popular crimson and buff colourings. The smartest of all his wares are the soft-soled leather patch-work ones in suitable sizes for men, women and children. Each of the patches is gaily embroidered round the edges, and the whole is cunningly worked into designs and patterns. These are usually known as Kokand boots, from having been originally made there. An embroidered over-shoe with a stout sole accompanies this kind of boot, which is easily slipped off on entering a house.

In some by-lane the dyer's quarter is usually to be found, and in one the owner, with the sleeves of his robe rolled up, displays a pair of dyed arms, as he twists and wrings out of the large brass vats filled with indigo, red, green or yellow vegetable dye the skeins of silk or cotton or woven material entrusted to his skill, which he then proceeds to hang out to dry on projecting pieces of wood placed there for the purpose, thus adding the appearance of gay streaming banners to his street.

Bokhara is also famed for its cutlery, in the shape of small pointed knives that are universally carried in a wooden or leather case thrust into the girdle. The handles are often elaborately decorated and inlaid with silver and turquoises, and the steel is so finely tempered as seldom to require sharpening.

The tobacco stalls, too, form a wonderful note of colour. A heap of bright green snuff in the centre is flanked by gourd snuff-bottles dyed in every shade. The gourds are shaped while growing; some are left the natural buff colour and stencilled with patterns in black or red. Little carved bone stoppers prevent the powder from escaping, except when they are removed to permit of the owner sucking the snuff, which is the Turcoman way of enjoying tobacco. Perhaps alongside there may be a stall for the sale of rock-salt in pink blocks, which comes from a mine at Karshi, south of Samarkand, and also from one in the Nuratagh Hills. Salt is not so cheap as with us, and these blocks are a convenient and economical form in which to place the salt within reach of cattle, that they may lick it.

In the open squares one finds all sorts of small traders, their stock spread on the ground, shaded by a large square umbrella-like awning, the advantage of which is that its angle may be altered according to the position of the sun. In the gold and silver bazaars there is not much stock on hand, as most work is done to order, but often antique specimens can be picked up that have been bartered for pieces of modern design. The silver-work on the whole is coarse and the designs not attractive. Where finer work is required the silversmith has an ingenious method of improving the somewhat feeble light of their kerosene lamps. A glass globe is filled with water and placed between the lamp and the worker, a very ancient method now introduced to Europe as a novelty.

The silk bazaar, with its wonderful embroideries and velvets in colourings peculiar to Bokhara, also displays silk scarves of a texture unmatched for softness, woven in the natural colour of silk, and dyed in shades unknown to aniline, the secrets being handed down from father to son, chiefly by those of the Jewish community. Under the shade of some mulberry grove one may see these same scarves being woven on primitive looms, so different from the noisome manufactures that so-called civilization may bring. One of the many uses to which the hand-woven silks are turned is that of embroidering the wonderful crimson and green hangings in large rose pattern, worked in a solid stitch on a linen or cotton ground, in the finer pieces, so closely that the fabric is almost invisible, and probably the origin of the rose design emanated from Persia. No piece is ever fully completed, to avoid bringing ill luck on the worker.

There is a charming legend which narrates the origin of silk. When the prophet Job was afflicted, the archangel Gabriel was sent down with a hundred thousand angels to remove his riches, and still the prophet praised on. Disease was then sent into his body, which was covered with worms, and still the prophet praised on. By command of God the archangel Gabriel was ordered to obtain water. He smote the earth with his wings, when there gushed forth a spring of living water in which Job was ordered to bathe. As he did so, his sores were healed and his flesh was made whole like that of a little child. The fountain remained and was known as the Sea of Life, in which all who bathed became perfect in soul and body. The worms which fell from the body of Job swam out of the water and climbed into a mulberry-tree, where they ate of the leaves, and in order to conceal themselves and thus avoid punishment for their sin, wrapped themselves up in coverings which they spun, and these coverings are called cocoons, from which they escaped in another disguise.

The rugs woven in home looms of the wool of the country are famed for colour and design, while the weaving of the saddle-bags shows a fineness that cannot be surpassed. Their designs likewise are handed down through generations and are never altered, and it is by the fame of its rugs that the name of Bokhara is best known to the Western world.

XII

Bokhara the Noble (continued)

A Sign of Luck – A Surgical Operation – Caracul
Bazaar – Officialdom – Past Cruelties – A
State Ceremonial – A Women's Hospital

As the king said, so was it done,
And to the Mosque my lord passed on.

When Tamerlane transferred his capital to Samarkand the mosques of Bokhara fell on evil days. Unlike those of Egypt and Turkey, they are all open-fronted and deeply recessed, the recess forming a shelter for the worshippers, and though they are now in a somewhat ruinous condition many fine tiles still remain upon their walls. The tiled façade terminates in small towers at each side, and on the top of these may frequently be seen a stork's nest, a sign of luck, and as such the birds are almost regarded as sacred and are left undisturbed in their exalted sphere.

The older mosques, instead of having a fountain or basin as part of the sacred buildings, are usually built beside a huge tank, where the necessary ablutions before worship may be performed. The tank is surrounded by trees whose spreading branches form a grateful shade to the citizens, who flock there in crowds to meet their friends. I used always to look upon those shaded terraces as the clubs of Bokhara. Various tea-houses, eating-places and barbers' shops are at hand to cater for all wants; and what picturesque groups are to be seen there, sitting cross-legged on rugs or low seats, regardless of any stranger in their midst. The barbers are, as of old in our country, the surgeons of the community, and a common sight is the operation for guinea-worm. An incident which I witnessed illustrates the dangers which lurk in the tank water. A barber was operating on a patient afflicted with guinea-worm (*Filaria*), a slender elongated para-site producing tumours, usually found in the legs. The worm is removed by being turned round a stick, while gentle massage is applied: a slow process, as only a few inches are extracted in one day, and if the worm be severed in the operation the fragment left sets up blood-poisoning and the patient usually dies. In the case observed the worm after removal was thrown into the tank! It is only necessary to add that infection is normally due to foul drinking water, the young worms finding their first host in minute water animals. A protest on my part was quite ineffect-ive, the barber pointing out that other worms had already been flung into the tank.

The presence of this disease was known even in the time of Anthony Jenkinson, an envoy from Queen Elizabeth to the Court of Tamerlane, for he notes in his diary: 'There is a little river running through the middes of the saide citie, but the water thereof most unholsome, for it breedeth sometimes in men that drink thereof, and especially in them that be not there borne, a worme of an ell long, which lieth commonly in the legge betwixt the flesh and the skinne, and is pluckt out about the ancle with great art and cunning, the Surgeones being much practised therein, and if shee breake in plucking out the partie dieth, and every day she commeth oute about an inch, which is rolled up and so worketh till she be all oute.'

The uses to which the water of these tanks is put are endless, including washing of all kinds, vegetable, mineral and animal, while the water, being partially stagnant, has a permanent green scum on its surface. It is changed about once a fortnight, an excuse then for all the youth of the town to have quite a gala day and go and bathe. From these tanks comes the water supply of Bokhara, except in cases where householders are sufficiently fortunate to possess a well, so need one wonder at the prevalence of disease of all kinds? How descriptive are the following lines regarding water conditions in summer:

> Thou know'st how fierce
> In these last days the sun hath burned:
> That the green waters in the tanks
> Is to a putrid puddle turned:
> And the canal, that from the stream
> Of Samarcand is brought this way
> Wastes, and runs thinner every day.

There is a regular corps of water-carriers, each of whom has his own beat, distributing the supply from skins carried on their backs: one hundred skinfuls cost one rouble. Reckonings are kept by strokes chalked upon the wall of the adjacent mosque, a convenient 'jotter,' and private accounts are kept by notches made on the waterman's stick, or else by lines chalked on the door of the customer's house. All proceeds from the sale of water go to the municipality. In spite of the lack of good water Anthony Jenkinson thus describes the enforced temperance regulations at the time of his visit:

'And yet it is there forbidden to drinke any other thing than water and mare's milke, and whosoever is found to breake that law is whipped and beaten most cruelly through the open markets, and there are officers appointed for the same who have authoritie to goe into any man's house to search if he have either aquavita, wine, or *brage*, and finding the same doe breake the vessels, spoyle the drinke, and punish the masters of the house most cruelly, yea, and many times if they perceive, but by the breathe of a man that he hath drinke without further examination hee shall not escape their handes.'

The love of Bokhariots for their trees is shown by the care with which they are preserved, even when their removal might seem a necessity, such as when building a house. Rather than cut the tree down, the house is built around it – branches are led through the walls and over the roof, and the trunk very often acts as a door-post.

Bokhara is what may be called a 'sheepy' place. All the furs are sheep in various stages of growth, all the meat is sheep, and most of the cooking is done in sheep fat extracted from the tail, which is a flap of solid fat several inches thick, and takes the place of the oil or butter of other countries. It reminds one of the French girl's remark on her first visit to Scotland after several days scanning the bill of fare: '*Mouton, mouton, toujours mouton !*' The centre of the astrakhan fur trade is in the Kara-cul bazaar, as that is the name by which the fur is known in Central Asia. It is a two-storey building. On the upper one may be seen the buyers, walking up and down, while trying to effect a deal, and secret offers are made by pressure of the hands beneath the very long sleeves of the *khalats*.

Representatives are to be found from all the chief European markets – London, Paris, Berlin, Leipzig, Moscow and

Constantinople. The lambs of various ages, from a day old and upwards, are kept on the ground floor or court, and when sold are then slaughtered, the skins roughly cured with salt or alum, and then hung out to dry upon the stone wall balconies of the courtyard. Black is most in demand, though grey and white have a sale. The skins of the very young lambs show a texture equal to the finest plush and are known to the trade as bébé lamb, or breitswanz. I saw one collection of skins belonging to a very wealthy Sart merchant, worth £2000, and this was only a two days' purchase. Some skins that may almost be called 'freaks' fetch enormous prices. One skin alone had cost £600 because of its three shades of colouring – black, white and brown – and the curl was peculiarly regular. Another was reckoned at a high figure because of what was supposed to be the word 'Allah' formed in Arabic characters, in brown on a white ground. Some attempts have been made to export these caracul sheep to other countries possessing apparently the same conditions of existence, but I understand the results have not been satisfactory. Even in Central Asia the radius where they are bred is a fairly limited one, and when the animals are removed from it the fur loses the special qualities for which it is famed, but no satisfactory reason for this has as yet been discovered.

Among the buildings the most noticeable is that of 'the Ark,' or Citadel, built in the twelfth century by Alp Arslan. Surrounded by a high crenellated wall twenty feet thick, it is approached from the Registan, or market-place, by an important-looking gateway flanked by two round towers. Inside this entrance are guard-houses, and on a low platform for two hours every morning sits the Kushbeg, or Vizier, to hear complaints and redress grievances.

Another official who 'keeps the conscience of the king' is the Reis, who sees to the moral state of the inhabitants. Whip in hand, he parades the town, and if necessary administers summary punishment. The powers of this modern Paul Pry are only limited by the Emir and his Prime Minister, who give him absolute jurisdiction in an office which is supposed to maintain the laws of the Koran.

On the top of the gateway of the Citadel, 'In the great window of the gate, looking into the Registan,' is a clock made in the last century by an Italian – Giovanni Orlando. He had been kidnapped and sold as a slave. The then Emir, Nasrullah by name, hearing of him, sent for him in order to gratify his passion for all mechanical work. Orlando offered to set up a clock on the gateway of the Ark on condition that he was given his liberty. The clock was made and set up, and Orlando became a free man, but having the misfortune to offend the Emir, he ordered him to be imprisoned and only to be pardoned on the condition that he renounced his faith and become a Mahometan. This he refused to do, and the Emir, unmindful of his mechanical gifts, had him beheaded.

This same Nasrullah was the Emir who so brutally murdered Conolly and Stoddart in 1841. These men were sent by the East India Company on a peaceful mission to the Emir of Bokhara in 1837. He imprisoned them for over three years, during which time they experienced the horrors of Bokharan dungeons and were, it is said, finally killed by being flung from the top of the minaret, Minar Katan, 210 feet high, a favourite mode of execution, and practised until thirty years ago.

Immediately outside the Citadel is the armoury. A collection of mounted fire-arms, some in bronze, included artistic pieces of metal-work, but all were much more suited to a museum than for use in active warfare. In 1910 the guard were quite in keeping: hardly two were clothed alike, and many wore discarded British uniforms of our Indian army. By 1912 great strides had been made in the clothing department. All were clothed alike, smartly turned out in white Russian belted shirts, breeches, and high boots, with every appearance of having been drilled. As Russia sees to the protection of its states, anything done in the military line must merely be a concession to the pride of a ruler.

I had cherished a vain hope of being able to effect an entrance into the Ark, but I believe that any Englishman would have difficulty in obtaining permission, and the fact of being a woman made the conclusion foregone.

Still, although not admitted to the Ark, I was able to see the Emir on his way to attend the Friday service at an adjoining mosque. From motives, I suppose, of personal safety, or from a wish to avoid favouritism, the place of worship is changed every week, and the name of the mosque to be honoured is kept a secret. On this occasion the secret leaked out, as secrets will, and by an early hour in the morning I took up my station in front of the Ark. For something like three hours I waited, the crowd always increasing, though kept at a respectful distance, and most kindly I was allowed to stand in the front row to permit of photographing. I must have seen all the officials of the state pass in and out of the gateway that morning – figures in cloth of gold and silver, and the richest brocades and velvets, a veritable kaleidoscope of colour. One quaint little group of gorgeously apparelled retainers bore aloft the Emir's silver seat, and others followed carrying his further requirements into the mosque. These were no doubt the equivalent of the knights and squires and lords and grooms of hereditary offices of our Court in mediaeval times. All this worked up to the chief figure in this magnificent state pageant, the Emir himself, mounted on a superb black horse. It was covered with a gorgeously embroidered saddle-cloth and trappings of gold, while the very stout rider was not less resplendent in robes of cloth of gold. Having been assisted to dismount, he retired into the mosque, and then almost simultaneously the vast throng outside removed their shoes and knelt on prayer-rugs to perform their devotions, as, owing to the smallness of the mosque, only a limited number could gain admittance. It was one of the most impressive spectacles that could be imagined, added to which the vivid colouring of that picturesque crowd made a sight that can never be forgotten.

On one side of the square, in front of the Ark, is the largest mosque in Bokhara, called Masjid-i-Jami, capable of holding 10,000 in its courtyard. Not far off is the round tower called Minar Katan, about two hundred feet in height, and of exquisite proportions, built of brick in stamped-out designs, with an occasional inlay of bottle-green tiles. It had the unfortunate distinction of being used until comparatively recent times as a means of execution, criminals being flung from its summit.

The two most modern public buildings are the public baths and the hospital, the latter erected by the Tsar of Russia. The first was opened in 1897, thanks to the generosity of the Chief Justice, and is in the form of Turkish baths. The second was built by the Tsar Alexander II. in 1910 as a thank-offering for the escape of his son, the late Tsar, when an attempt was made on his life in Japan, and very considerately took the form of a hospital for women. Although far from possessing the modern standard of hospital requirements, at least it offers care and kindness, sanitary treatment and medical skill. I travelled with the Russian matron, an intelligent, capable woman, so on going to see her she displayed with pride her 'show' cases. One epileptic had gashed herself terribly with a knife, and the horrible gaping wound under iodoform treatment was rather revolting to look at. Tumours seemed as common as cockroaches. There was not one nightgown among the lying-down cases, and sheets were sparse, which perhaps did not matter so much, as most of the patients seemed half huddled up in their day garments. Even under such conditions the hospital with its dispensary must be an untold boon to the suffering women of Bokhara.

From far and near they throng to receive the needed medical treatment, with an implicit faith in the power of the European to cure – a faith which is not misplaced when one realizes the primitive mode of doctoring in vogue amongst their own people. The list of contents of the witches' cauldron in *Macbeth* would aptly describe the pharmacopoeia of a Bokharan medico. One instance came under my own observation. A patient suffering from blindness was advised to swallow the eyes of a hawk in order that its keenness of vision might to some extent be imparted to the sufferer. A common Sart superstition is that when anyone is ill they throw a garment belonging to the sick one on the road in hope of someone picking it up and thus taking away the ailment.

In spite of apparent drawbacks to a healthy existence in Bokhara the Arabic geographer Ibn Hankal thus notes his impression: 'I have often been at Kohendiz, the ancient castle of Bokhara, I have cast my eyes around, and never have I seen a verdure more fresh and more abundant, or of wider extent. This green carpeting mingled in the horizon with the azure of blue skies. The simple verdure served as a sort of ornamental off-set to the towns contained in it. Numerous country seats decorated the simplicity of the fields. Hence I am not surprised that of all the inhabitants of Khorasan none attain a more advanced age than those of Bokhara.'

XIII

Thus Spake the Interpreter

A Garden City – Indifferent Hotels – A Pious Cook – A Man of Many Words – A Lively Night – A Sigh of Relief

> And those to whom he spoke remember'd well,
> And on the words however light would dwell;
> None knew, nor how, nor why, but he entwined
> Himself perforce around the hearer's mind.

A perfectly uninteresting train journey of eight hours from Bokhara (which is only 150 miles away), through more or less desert country until entering the fertile lands watered by the Zerafshan, is the penalty exacted from those who would visit Samarkand in the modern fashion. Situated on a western spur of the Thian Shan Mountains, its elevation of 2000 feet gives a feeling of exhilaration on emerging from the handsome stone-built station, two and a half miles distant from the modern Russian town. A collection of drinking booths and huts somewhat detract from its architectural pretensions and give one a false impression of what is to follow; but the traveller, notwithstanding, cannot fail to be struck on his droshky drive with the broad avenues of silver poplar, black elm, and acacia, whose roots are laved by gurgling streams and whose leaves fan soft breezes around the various houses, residential and commercial, that are built amid their shade. The Russo-Chinese Bank, set in a garden that anyone might envy, is one of the most prominent, and its fortunate manager lives in the storey above his business accommodation. The various public buildings associated with the life of a Russian town are to be found on those stately avenues, as well as shops for the sale of European goods.

Ibn Hankal gives an account of Samarkand as it appeared to him in the tenth century – so far back does its civilization extend:

> There are here many villas and orchards, and very few of the palaces are without gardens, so that if a person should go to the Kohnedez, and from that look around, he would find that the villas and palaces were covered, as it were, with trees; and even the streets and shops and banks of the streams are all planted with trees.

How applicable is this description at the present day.

There are various hotels, more or less indifferent, and they constantly seem to change hands. The one in which I lodged was primitive, none too clean, and the bedroom recalls a vision of a broken-springed mattress, a rickety table, and one chair. On Easter Day, when no work is done, the landlady, although of Jewish race, did not fail to observe a Church festival in this manner, but she very kindly consented to boil some rice and milk for my dinner; her cuisine even under ordinary circumstances was limited, and only extended to one meal a day. It usually consisted of *pilau* and *compote* of dried apricots called *pish-mish*, but once she gave me roast ox tongue; such an odd dish, and only to be recommended as being easier to cut than the usual fragments of tough broiled meat.

The specimens daily served up almost made me feel inclined to become a Seventh Day Advent Christian, whose theology, according to the Interpreter, might be bad, but whose gastronomy is quite correct. I believe part of their creed is to start vegetarian restaurants.

In spite of the culinary failings of the landlady, the Interpreter never ceased praising her for her good deeds. 'She is a very pious woman,' he kept repeating, till I discovered that her piety chiefly consisted in giving him Passover food without charging him anything for it, 'chicken bouillon,' which he said was 'heavenly,' and Passover cakes. I even heard him murmur: 'She may get to heaven by an easier way.' I could not forbear remarking to him that I wondered his conscience allowed him to accept of it, for at the hotel in Ashkabad, also kept by Jews, when they invited him to share their Passover meals for payment he said: 'My Passover is Christ.' He had an astonishing gift for the display of long words. I was washing out my saucepan one day and asked him if he thought it was clean. 'Bacteriorically I should say it was.' One could hardly dare to admire even a tree for fear of the dissertation that would then follow on 'the science and symmetry of nature.' With all his fine expressions he was hopeless when it came to practical work. I once tried to send off two parcels by post and wherever we stopped the parcels were taken to the post office and as unfailingly brought back. Finally at Khokand we saw the last of them, but not until after he had made seven efforts to dispose of them. It became at last almost a joke, if it had not been annoying, and if I said how troublesome it was, 'Ah, but you remember, the Psalmist says, man is born to trouble.' I feel sure now this wail must have been wrung from David under similar trials.

He distinguished himself on another occasion by leaving our passports behind, which meant an absolute block to further progress till they were recovered. He covered himself with glory, in his own estimation, on one occasion when we arrived at a railway junction at one-thirty in the morning and had to wait there till daylight. I managed to secure a corner in which to lie down in the ladies' waiting-room, but not for ten minutes was there peace, women coming and going all the time, and when no one else was banging the door it was done by the keeper of the room herself, who delivered long harangues in Russian to any chance listener. It made no difference to pretend one was asleep, for, when all other pastime failed, she leant over me to arrange her hair in the mirror which hung above my chosen place of rest: a hideous pock-marked female with her head tied up in the usual Russian handkerchief. The Interpreter had a still livelier night, for he fell in with the priest from a neighbouring parish who was drunk and had come to draw his salary at the station, though why he should have chosen one A.M. to do so I never found out. The Interpreter fell to words with him as he declined to join him in his drinking bout, and the priest then insisted on seeing me and made for the door of the waiting-room. This accounted for various scuffling movements and door-banging with which I was favoured.

The Interpreter's further account was too funny, as I could see his conduct in the affair was much mixed with cowardice. 'And do you call yourself a follower of the meek and lowly Jesus?' he asked.

The priest still retained sufficient glimmer of consecratedness to cross himself at these words, and again demanded to see me that he might give me his blessing.

'And is not sleep the best blessing she can have?' retorted the Interpreter, and with that he called assistance, and two porters fell on their knees and implored the priest to let me be. He then took the arm of the Interpreter and staggered up and down the platform with him until he was tired out and ready to freshen up the morning with five or six glasses of brandy, which I rather gathered the Interpreter had not the courage to refuse to share, as by this time the *chef de police* had arrived, and in order to secure the one droshky the place had to offer, the Interpreter said he had to treat him to the customary morning refreshment.

On any railway journey by night I always gave the Interpreter instructions that if I had the carriage to myself he was to tip the conductor at the end of the journey. A lady arrived in the early hours of the morning and tried to get into my carriage, but unsuccessfully, so on asking him afterwards what became of her, he replied quite gravely: 'As she was not bellicose she sat up!' He did get hold of the most extraordinary words, and gave himself out as a teacher of English. He very nearly equalled a Lett I once had as guide. He was endeavouring to describe the opening of an early saint's grave, which he did in the following words: 'Man had him grab oop and he was not'ing but sand'!

I shall quote from my diary letter the closing scene with the Interpreter. With a sigh of relief I had said farewell to him: 'The Interpreter was ordered by the police to quit Moscow in twelve hours, as it appears no Jew is allowed to live there except under special conditions, and an hotel harbouring one is liable to a fine amounting to 500 roubles. Of course he was furious that all his protestations of Christianity were of no avail.'

XIV

The Golden Road to Samarkand

Happy Crowds – A Cruel Custom – A Camel Caravan – The Registan – Al Fresco Meals – Fortune-Telling – Moonlight

> I am fevered with the sunset,
> I am fretful with the land,
> For the wander-thirst is on me,
> And my soul's in Samarkand.

It has always seemed to me that the true interpretation of the golden road to Samarkand is to be found there on a spring morning, all aglow with a sunshine that is indeed foreign to our eyes, produced by the clearness of that wonderfully translucent atmosphere, where even every atom of dust helps to radiate a golden glory; it is difficult to imagine and equally impossible to describe, but such atmospheric conditions are one of the charms of that attractive land.

Chaffering, happy-go-lucky crowds swing along, full of business though not busy, accepting the chances that the gold may fall into their laps: alike hopeful whether it be for that day or fate send it on another.

In raiment of rags or in richest robes all pass along, some aloft on the humps of the long processions of Bactrian camels, that are laden with chests and bales of goods from the markets of India, or it may be from still farther East.

From neighbouring villages and hamlets come herds of cattle and calves, and flocks of sheep and lambs, while a crowd of merry little people are running hither and thither, driving the poor animals silly in their childish efforts to guide them. Mingled among the crowd are horses and donkeys, with one or more men and boys riding astride them, flanked by what I can only call bunches of fowls, which are hung head downwards in front of the saddle, or at the back of it, should that space not be already occupied by a second rider; indeed, wherever it is possible for a string to be suspended, there are hung those 'live long-legged beasties.' A black or grey shrouded bundle may occasionally be seen on the back of a donkey or pony, but try as one may, not a feature is visible behind the closely woven horsehair mesh of a woman's veil. Not being a lady of high degree, she is in this way permitted to see something of the 'fun of the fair.'

A peculiar custom is practised of slitting up the nostrils of donkeys when they are foals, with the idea that it permits the air to enter more freely into their lungs and thus allow them to breathe more easily. This mutilation gives a somewhat Mephistophelian cast of countenance to what is normally a wistful and rather pathetic one. The horses are of a small but hardy breed, and a load of lucerne which may allow of only the head and hoofs to be seen is accounted nothing. They are on the whole kindly treated, and decked with bead necklaces and strings of cowrie shells, coloured-wool tassels and neckbands of coils of wool, red, blue and yellow – sometimes the donkey's neck is swathed in all three – to which are appended oddments of brass ornaments: in addition, the riding animals have embroidered saddle-cloths, more or less large and rich according to the master's purse. These attentions are not altogether of a disinterested nature, for the evil eye has to be propitiated or dire misfortunes may befall a neglectful owner. These decorations are not omitted, indeed they are even augmented when the animal is harnessed to an *arba*, or native hooded cart. The driver sits in a most cramped position, huddled up on the horse's back, while his feet rest on the shafts. It is amazing how in such a confined position he can have any control of the animal, but runaway horses are rarely seen; low feeding and heavy loads have a wonderfully subduing effect where such quadrupeds are concerned.

All are bent on one object, which is that of attending the markets. These may be held either in the streets or on open spaces allowed for the purpose; that for the sale of fodder is to be conveniently found on entering the town, under the shadow of the famous ruins of the Bibi Khanum Mosque, and bundles of lucerne and a species of tare change hands with the deliberation that is entailed by the universal system of bargaining.

A gathering cloud of dust and the musical tinkling of camel bells betoken the arrival of a caravan, whose loads are deposited according to the nature of the merchandise carried. If of a soft nature it is usually carried in striped black-and-white sacks, made of undyed sheep's-wool; if the load be of the nature of wood or stones, that is accommodated in a species of wooden cradle made for the purpose. Each animal's head is tied to the tail of the one in front, and woe betide any man who causes alarm to such a string, the confusion and difficulty of straightening it out again is so great, and adds to the burden of grievances which a camel always seems to bear.

Whether it is being subjected to the process of loading or unloading it is immaterial, this is done to the accompaniment of grunts and growls and raucous roars that awaken little sympathy from the human onlookers. Even for an animal the charm of its youth soon fades, and it speedily joins the ranks of its wrinkled and careworn-looking ancestors.

Let us now follow the crowd to that wonder spot of Samarkand – the Registan. Surely no town in the world can boast of such a market-place. About four hundred feet square, it is roughly paved and is surrounded on three sides by a trio of wonder mosques of the world.

As one emerges from a narrow street and enters this vast space it seems at first sight almost to give one a sense of unreality, so totally unlike is it to anything one has ever seen or imagined.

The delicate proportions of slender minarets and fluted domes are combined with a wonderful strength in the general effect of those dazzlingly beautiful coloured façades.

Those mosques, though Eastern in conception, have a nobility of proportion and virility of execution that reveal a blend of some other race, or perhaps, more correctly speaking, they were the work of a people whose decadence was still remote.

Lord Curzon, in his book, *Russia in Central Asia*, gives a wonderful picture. 'The Reghistan,' he says, 'was originally and is still, even in its ruins, the noblest public square in the world. I know nothing in the East approaching it in massive simplicity and grandeur, and nothing in Europe, save perhaps, on a humble scale, the Piazza di San Marco at Venice, which can even aspire to enter the competition. No European spectacle indeed can adequately be compared with it, in our inability to point to an open space in any Western city that is commanded on three of its four sides by Gothic cathedrals of the finest order. For it is clear that the medresse of Central Asian Mahomedanism, in both its architectural scope and design, is a lineal counterpart and forerunner of the Minster of the West. Instead of the intricate sculpture and tracery crowning the pointed archways of the Gothic front, we see the enamelled tiles of Persia, framing the portal of stupendous magnitude. For the flanking minster towers or spires are substituted two soaring minarets. The central lantern of the West is anticipated by the Saracenic dome; in lieu of artificial colour thrown through tinted panes, from the open heavens shine down the azure of the Eastern sky and the glory of the Eastern sun. What Samarkand must have been in its prime, when these great fabrics emerged from the mason's hands, intact and glittering with all the effulgence of the rainbow, their chambers crowded with students, their sanctuaries thronged by pilgrims, and their corporations endowed by kings, the imagination can still make some endeavour to depict.'

The first of those mosques was built in 1421 by Ulea Beg, the grandson of Tamerlane. He was a man devoted to the science of mathematics and astronomy, and, as was most appropriate, in the *medresse*, or college, associated with his name there were taught those subjects which were of such interest to him. It contains twenty-four rooms, now, alas, in a sadly ruined condition, and I fear the teaching has also fallen from its high standard.

The brick façade is inlaid with blue tiles (the secret of whose colouring was lost even by the sixteenth century), and inset at regular intervals are windows whose panes are not of glass, but white marble fretwork, as is so often found in Indian architecture, shedding a soft light peculiarly grateful to the eyes in contrast to the glare outside of a hot summer sun.

In point of age comes next the mosque on the north side, called Tillah-Kari, built by Imam-Kuli-Khan in 1641. Perhaps of all the three when new it must have been the most gorgeous. It is 400 feet long and 100 feet in height at the great centre portal, or *piktash* as it is called. All is inlaid with blue tiles in formal designs, whose groundwork was gold covered with a thin glaze in order to protect them from weather conditions. How this golden surface must have sparkled and glittered in the bright Eastern sunshine!

For an imposing frontage, to my mind the mosque called Shir-dar is worthy of first place, built also by Imam-Kuli-Khan in 1648. He covered the entire façade with an inlay of blue tiles; the domes of the building were fluted and the minarets were inlaid with in all-over design in blue on a cream brick ground; while each corner of the centre portion of the façade is finished with slender inlaid pillars. At the upper corners of the majestic portal, inlaid in blue and yellow tiles, are the Persian emblems, the lion (which looks more like a tiger) and the sun, giving the name of Shir-dar to the mosque, which means 'lion-bearing.' The minarets at each side have been a subject of much discussion, being even likened to the leaning Tower of Pisa, and either glory is given to the architect for his genius in so balancing them, or else earth-quakes have been blamed for so displacing them. Personally I could only see that the minarets were perfectly upright and that the optical delusion was caused by the centre part of the building being considerably narrower at the top than at the foundation, and probably the original idea of the architect in this was to cause an apparently greater width to the façade by a false assumption that the minarets sloped outwards.

At first sight one does not really grasp the full height of the mosques, and it is only by the transference of the eye to the crowd below, which makes its component parts of well-nigh midget size, that the full dignity of the elevation can be appreciated. And how can one describe that picturesque crowd, and where could one find such an absolute kaleidoscope of colouring? It made me feel all the time as if it were part of some gorgeous pageant out of *The Arabian Nights*.

The older men wore nothing more sombre than red-striped *khalats*, and the younger members donned such gay ones, blue, pink, green, yellow, in Bokharan rainbow designs. Vividly I remember the robe of one 'knut'; it had bold forked patterns in black and yellow crossed by broad lines of magenta!

The men all wear beards, and when age approaches openly dye them with henna. A wizened face and pink beard is a sorry sight! The turban is universally worn by the Sart population wound round a stitched skull-cap, with one end of the muslin hanging down coquettishly on the left side, and among the snowy white ones an occasional green one is to be seen, betokening that its wearer has made the far and meritorious journey to Mecca.

Such gay butterflies are the men, for women are seldom or never seen out of doors, and if ever they are met, one finds them from the head downwards smothered in a dark-coloured or grey alpaca coat-like garment with elongated sleeves, the cuffs of which are fastened at the edge of the back of the coat, and their fringed ends trail in the dust.

If we visit the Registan in the early morning we shall find trade brisk, and the morning avocation going on of barbers shaving heads beneath the mosque walls. Food is appetizingly set out on brass trays in the form of fried meat cakes, and bowls of rice of the national *pillau*, while little braziers are kept alight by means of wisps of grass and twigs and serve to broil fragments of meat, called *shashlik*, on skewers.

For the less affluent customers there was *omelette aux fines herbes*, which is made in a copper pan about one and a half feet in diameter. It is sold in slices, of which two can be had for the equivalent of a farthing, but under the more attractive names of a *merree*, a *doob*, or a *tenga*. Their exact value I never quite mastered, but these are brass or copper coins of a local mintage in common use in Samarkand and Bokhara. Hard-boiled eggs were also sold, dyed red and blue, from which the idea of our Easter eggs is supposed to have been derived.

Sweets were very popular with old and young – even though mutton fat does not sound a tempting foundation – under the form of pastes made of fruit, and candies of almonds and pistachio nuts in sugar coverings brightly coloured.

The bakers, who are very clever at their trade, also make a cake of flour, honey, and pistachio nuts; perhaps somewhat sweet and lacking flavour to the jaded palates of the West.

When the brass trays are emptied of their contents, the folding stands which support them have merely to be closed and the food-seller walks off with his tray and stand – a simple and inexpensive method of keeping a restaurant. I always fancied that, like crossing-sweepers at home, there must have been a recognized code of honour as to a particular stance, but probably the regulation may only have been that of the early bird.

In spring the stems of uncooked rhubarb are freely chewed along with spring onions; these last are sold in bundles, often by children, who delight in arranging them on their heads like caps, the bulbs forming a ball-like fringe.

As regards native food, Dr Lansdell in his book on Central Asia says: 'They [the natives] eat no pork, and some eat neither hares nor rabbits, though they are not forbidden. Camel, I believe, is forbidden, and in Bokhara not eaten, nor are horses, but the Kirghese eat both. Goats would appear to be not much used for food in Bokhara. We heard there is a porridge of rice and milk, and of *lapsha*, a sort of vermicelli. To these may be added fowls, ducks, geese, and, near the Oxus, pheasants. It must not be supposed, however, that the people in general feast on these dainties daily. The rich live on *pilau*. The well-to-do families live on bread and tea daily, but *pilau* on Thursday and Sunday. Workmen, carters, etc., have *pilau* daily, and shopkeepers eat *pilmain*, or pieces of meat on a skewer, and not all off prime joints, but some of liver and inferior parts. They drink a good deal – in summer ice and honey. The poor make soup out of wheat and other grain, and the poorest eat sorghum.'

The bread-sellers wandered around, bearing trays cleverly balanced on the palm of the hand: a very ancient method, as it is frequently depicted on the walls of the tombs of ancient Egypt. The bread is in the form of large round flat scones of a spongy dough, while the Persian bread is of much the same consistency, but made in long narrow strips and sold by the yard or some equivalent measure.

In 1497 Baber thus writes in his *Memoirs*:

'Samarkand is a wonderfully elegant city. One of its distinguishing peculiarities is, that each trade has its own bazaar; so that different trades are not mixed together in the same place. The established customs and regulations are good. The bakers and shops are excellent, and the cooks are skilful.'

With the approach of warm days comes the ice-cream man, minus the cream. The deftness with which he makes his ices is a marvel to behold. With a block of frozen snow in front of him, he scrapes some of this on to a small brass platter; a ladle of raisin syrup is poured over this and then mixed up with a flat wooden spoon, and the ice is made and ready for the never-ending crowd of old and young around his stall proffering in exchange strange little odd-shaped native coins that were always promptly dropped into a bowl of water. I cannot think sanitary reasons could have suggested this action, but more probably it arose from a fancied sense of greater security for the coins themselves. Not far off I discovered the stall for the sale of this syrup. Seeing the corpses of brown, black, and white goats, minus the heads, all laid out on a shelf, I had the curiosity to examine further this mysterious row. From perambulating living quadrupeds a few days previously they had become the receptacle for honey and syrup! '*Bon appetit*,' thought I; and here is a solution of the riddle: 'Out of the strong came forth sweetness.'

The trade of fortune-tellers is much encouraged. So wishful one day to pacify a persistent loafer I tried his skill. He tossed some brass dice-looking pieces, said I was born on a lucky day, and in five days or so I would be at another place, and all would be well with my journey, and in a few days I should have a letter from home; so he did not risk his reputation much on my account.

On Fridays a mullah was always to be found preaching outside one of the mosques. One in particular I remember who gesticulated excitedly, and his voice rose and fell as he loudly declaimed to a kneeling crowd of listeners. He was said to be repeating tales and maxims out of the Koran, to which his hearers loudly assented, nodded their heads approvingly to his remarks, and responded to the collection which was made at the close. Another little group would be seated in some corner listening to a band of native musicians recounting tales of national history and heroism to the accompaniment of a rather primitive-looking instrument called the *dutara*, similar in shape to a guitar but rather smaller; the two strings are usually of fine wire and are played by hand. There is another and rather more elaborate instrument whose notes are drawn out with the bow, and for dance music a tambourine is played over a fire of coals in order that the heat may draw out the tone and thus still better help to accentuate the time. The more ambitious forms of bands consist of drums beaten loudly to the accompaniment of weird notes emitted from immensely long brass trumpets – truly lung-testers.

Games of chess and dominoes and also some very elementary forms of gambling are the diversion of the tea-house frequenters. Such ramshackle sheds those usually are, placed if possible by a ditch of running water, and where there is this asset, square-shaped, string-laced seats like bedsteads are placed across it, upon which are spread felt mats and skins, and on those the customers sit cross-legged and enjoy their light refreshment while gossiping to their hearts' content. I had several acquaintances in the Registan who were always ready to proffer their services as guides or inter-preters; a feeble game this last, as their Russian was so limited; however, their disinterested good nature and honesty never failed them. One day I tried to get some old brass, especially the brass and copper jugs then being fast superseded by enamelled iron ones. The moment the word *starre*, which means 'old,' was pronounced, like a flash it went round the bazaars, and every kind of suitable and unsuitable article was produced. Among them I found an ancient sling projectile found on the Afrosiab, made of a substance that has almost the appearance of cement, with spiral rounds cut or moulded on it. Brass candlesticks of a practical shape with a large flat base seemed to appear on all sides, but among the many it was almost impossible to find a pair; being hand-made, no two are ever formed alike. While surrounded by an interested crowd watching the bargaining I found my back being gently prodded. I looked round, and here was the spout of a dilapidated teapot trying to draw attention. I felt that the proper place for it was the china-mender, a stall that never failed to have customers; and marvellous menders some of those men were; surrounded by fragments of tea-bowls and handleless and spout-less teapots, success never seemed to fail to crown their efforts at clasping, glueing and cementing, and even making metal spouts or tips. Either the owners got attached to their 'tchai' bowls or they are by nature conservative in their dislike of changes, but some of the specimens seemed hardly to warrant so much labour expended on them.

One day when purchases assumed abnormal proportions I had to try to find a droshky in which to return home. Cries of *'Ariba!'* were soon resounding, reminding one of an evening after a theatre at home, and all those kind natives set to work to do their best to get one. One finally came along, but it was already occupied by two Sarts. One of my friends yelled *'Haidee!'* The driver stopped, and involuntarily one of the Sarts pulled out a cotton bag which did duty for a purse, and was preparing to pay the fare, but realizing that he was to be turned out, he refused to go. Howls and yells of execration at him then ensued, in which the driver joined. The Sarts were not to be outdone, and the row was appeased only by my begging that they might be allowed to finish their drive.

I once spent a festival season at Samarkand, the Orthodox Easter and the Jewish Passover. Easter was ushered in at eleven P.M. Bells jangled and guns were fired until three A.M. to inaugurate fully a week of complete idleness. No business of any kind was done. We had holidays to celebrate the commencement and holidays to celebrate the close, and for fear of any possible blank days between that might demand work, we had the birthday of one of the Royal Family. As a Russian truly remarked to me: 'There is no lack of time or land in Russia.'

One striking feature of the rejoicing was that all the way-side trees in the native city were hung with covered bird-cages, and these were even suspended across the roadways like lamps. The occupants of the cages were quails, and it is a fashionable amusement of the gilded youths to have quail fights, the sporting instinct that under other skies would keep a pack of hounds. This also finds an outlet in the mediaeval sport of hawking, and it is not uncommon to see in the bazaars a falconer with a hawk perched upon his gloved hand, often a fine-looking, light-speckled bird, with its cruel eyes blinking in the sunshine, its legs tethered by a red silk cord, and a couple of small silver bells attached to the collar encircling its neck.

My closing remembrance of the Registan is by moonlight: the busy crowds had vanished, there was not a sound to be heard, in the silver light every line and curve of minaret and dome stood out, the sense of time seemed annihilated, and that 'Moon of Paradise' was the link that united the present with the past:

> Now glowed the firmament
> With living sapphires; Hesperus, that led
> The starry host, rode brightest, till the moon,
> Rising in clouded majesty, at length
> Apparent queen unveil'd her peerless light,
> And o'er the dark her silver mantle threw.
>
> MILTON

XV

Of Old Forgotten Far-Off Things

*Alexander the Great – His Capital – Undirected
Excavations – A Russian Collector – Bibi
Khanum – Her Palace – A Royal Wedding*

Amid the long and chequered history of Samarkand three names
stand out pre-eminently as dominating personalities in its making.
They are Alexander the Great, Bibi Khanum, Tamerlane's Chinese
wife, and Tamerlane himself.

The first is familiarly, and one might even say affectionately,
alluded to at the present day as Iskander Macedonsky by the
present inhabitants of his dominion. The cruelties of conquest are
long forgotten, and almost a halo of distinction has been trans-
mitted from the conqueror to the conquered in the claiming
possession of whatever be the link that binds them to such a hero.
In their estimation he has reached the regions of a romance that
has gradually been evolved out of his heroic deeds. His acts of
valour are alone remembered and are the theme of the modern
minstrels, who twang out the memory of them, not, indeed, on a
ten-stringed instrument of praise, but on a very primitive lute of
two, and merit is ascribed to him in such accumulative measure
that even allowing for Eastern imagery would well-nigh astonish
the subject of it himself. Should we wish to trace some genuine

connection with that mighty emperor in his former capital we must wend our way a short distance outside the present town to an isolated hill called the Afrosiab, which was undoubtedly the site of the capital of Sogdiana, founded by Alexander the Great, and where still exist foundations of what must have been for those days a strong place of defence. Surrounded by a natural gully, this defence has been further taken advantage of by deepening and widening the fosse. The lines of the citadel walls may still be traced in such portions as are made of burned brick; but as at the present day, for most of such work sun-dried brick was the material chiefly employed, so that were it not for the chopped straw and grass with which it was liberally mixed I doubt if any foundations would now be visible. In this citadel Alexander held his Court and received the submission of the vanquished races of Sogdiana, and it was here too, it is said, that in a fit of drunken passion he slew his faithful general, Cleitus, to whom he owed his life when in a moment of great danger.

As mentioned by Skrine and Ross in *The Heart of Asia*: 'His career has left an indelible impression on the Oriental mind, which is slow to grasp new ideas but extremely tenacious of them when formed. He is associated throughout Islam with the "Two Horned" of the Koran, and his exploits are the daily theme of professional story-tellers in the market-places of Central Asia.'

On the hill itself, amid the mounds of rubbish and debris, are to be found specimens of whole and broken fragments of pottery and glass. There is no organized plan of excavation, and the natives dig as they like, without any scientific knowledge, so that for the one perfect specimen that may be unearthed many others are smashed in so doing. On one spot I gathered up the fragments of what had once been five glass bowls of classic shapes and treasured them as much for the exquisite iridescent colouring of the pieces as for their historic interest.

Living in Samarkand at the time of my visit was a Russian workman, a sign-painter by trade, who with his boy had spent six years in this work of digging, and having amassed a collection of about a thousand perfect and imperfect specimens of pottery, he was most anxious to find a purchaser for them. In spite of the lack of encouragement he was a real enthusiast, and worked for the love and interest in such discoveries. Notice was sent to him that I would like to see his collection. I found him arrayed in a black frock-coat and white tie waiting to receive me with due ceremony at the entrance to his house. He explained that his time was spent in digging, and where necessary piecing fragments of the pottery together, adding that it might be weeks or months sometimes before a piece was completed. His artistic bent also found scope in sketching the various buildings of note, some of which had considerable value in point of interest, as every now and again an earthquake rumbles along and reduces still more of those buildings to ruins. The pottery he ascribed to the fourteenth century, the glass was very much older; but quite possibly the pottery might be of an earlier date and undoubtedly, with few exceptions, was of native manufacture, though Persian influence was clearly visible in several of the pieces. They were chiefly interesting from the originality of design and the wonderful glaze achieved on such a very coarse medium. Five pieces of the collection were eventually secured for the South Kensington Museum, but, alas, the remainder were bought by the National Museum at Kiev, and one wonders what has now become of all the sign-painter's treasures.

Of the history of Bibi Khanum there are various conjectures, but it appears now to be generally accepted that she was the daughter of the Emperor of China and as such she most certainly introduced a Chinese influence in art at Court. Of whatever nationality, we know that she was the dearly loved wife of Tamerlane, and in the romance of her life she much resembles his descendant Shah Jehan and his adored Nurmahal, for whom was erected the most beautiful tomb the world has ever looked upon, with this added charm, that it remains as perfect as the day when Shah Jehan deposited his treasures therein, while it is only in a fragmentary condition that we can behold the magnificent memorial building of Bibi Khanum.

> I worshipped as I knelt before
> The Queen, the Woman, and the Saint.

Built most probably between 1385 and 1400 by her as a college, mosque and tomb, we can even picture her using part of it as a palace. In the zeal of Tamerlane's desire to convert his Chinese wife, did he have constructed the giant white marble Koran stand, that from her station behind the latticed windows she might learn to spell out the tenets of his faith?

Did this induce her finally to hand over the building to Tamerlane to be used as a mosque and college only, and to build a humbler tomb beside it for herself? We wonder.

The Koran stand is now removed from its original platform beneath the palace windows to the centre of the court to prevent its total destruction in case of earthquakes were the buildings to fall on it. Virtue is still supposed to emanate from it to those who can crawl beneath its nine short pillars. This act is supposed to grant the desires of childless women and to soothe the aches of aged men.

A traveller in 1770 mentions having seen the giant volume that once lay open upon it, for long at the page last read by Bibi Khanum; but its fate is now unknown.

The front of the building shows a recessed portal, sixty feet wide, and high in proportion, flanked by octagon minarets inlaid with tiles, in a kind of interlaced Greek-key pattern. Between them rises that magnificent turquoise-blue dome, whose colour more than holds its own with nature, and whose fragment is the first sight to greet a traveller as it stands out and above the greenery of this garden city. Convex and concave bricks, moulded into panels, and niches inlaid in colour, almost seem to mock at any difficulties that might arise in connection with the sense of proportion of such a building.

The earthquakes of 1897 played sad havoc, though there is still sufficient left to show us that in the realm of art there were giants in those days. The Russians have done a certain amount of preservation, but a great deal more might have been achieved, and much has gone that might have remained intact; the mere prohibition of removal of tiles is not sufficient when the material in which they are set is fast crumbling to dust. Where the various melon-shaped domes are concerned, cement moulded to the original form has been the medium employed, and this preserves any coloured portions left.

From various contemporary writers we can glean some idea of the appearance of Bibi Khanum, of which perhaps the description given by Don Ruy Gonsalez di Clavigo, the Spanish envoy from King Henry III. of Castile in 1403, presents the most vivid picture as she appeared at the wedding feast of Tamerlane's grandsons.

He relates that 'When the people were all arranged in order round the wall which encircled the pavilion, Cano, the chief wife of this lord, came forth to be present at the feast. She had on a robe of red silk, trimmed with gold lace, long and flowing. It had no waist, and fifteen ladies held up the skirt of it to enable her to walk. She wore a crested head-dress of red cloth, very high, covered with large pearls, rubies, emeralds, and other precious stones, and embroidered with gold lace; on the top of all there was a little castle, on which were three large and brilliant rubies, surmounted by a tall plume of feathers ... Her hair, which was very black, hung down over her shoulders, and they value black hair much more than any other colour. She was accompanied by three hundred ladies, of whom three held her head-dress when she sat down, lest it should tilt over. She had so much white lead on her face that it looked like paper, and this is put on to protect it from the sun, for when they travel in winter or in summer all great ladies put this on.'

There are three remarks in this passage that somehow seem to confirm the Chinese origin of this favoured wife of Tamerlane. From the description, she was unveiled in public, she had black hair, and she took care of her complexion in the manner prescribed by the Chinese from time immemorial (though I should doubt the statement of white lead), from which is derived our modern *papier poudré*.

Very roystering those feasts must have been. We read of their being kept up all night, of cart-loads of roast horse-meat being served on stamped skin platters, of camels with panniers of roast mutton to maintain the truly Gargantuan scale of supplies. Drinking was carried to such excess that 'some of the men fell down drunk before her; and this was considered very jovial, for they think there can be no pleasure without drunken men.' A drink of a more temperate character, perhaps consumed by the ladies, was called *bosat*, and was made of cream and sugar. Multitudes were fed as they came in crowds to gaze at the vast encampments of luxurious silken tents carpeted with the finest rugs that the native looms could produce, and divans spread with costliest furs and the softest of cushions. We also read that there were even windows in the tents, which show that they must have rather more resembled pavilions, and those were shrouded with silken nets to guard against intruders.

In the comparatively small-domed building at one corner of the great courtyard are said to lie the remains of this gorgeous being. Decked in her jewels, she was placed in a coffin made fast with golden nails, a prey to the first thief that had the courage to prise it open. Warning tales are handed down of the fate that overtook all who made the attempt.

XVI

Tamerlane the Magnificent

Tamerlane – His Power and Pomp – Wedding Feasts – Death and Funeral – Jeremiah's Prison – Tamerlane's Ghost

> Valiant Tamerlane, the man of fame,
> The man that in the forehead of his fortune
> Bears figures of renown and miracle.

Let us now gather up what links we can of the reign of Tamerlane; and it is amazing, considering that he lived as far back as the fourteenth century, that so much remains of those architectural adornments added by him to Samarkand, which he made his capital.

From comparative obscurity he raised it by art and education to world-wide renown; but now the light of its fame is darkened, the life of its busy colleges has ceased, its palaces have perished, and only the dead have been able to retain some semblance of their homes of rest.

Of Tamerlane we have many conflicting accounts – even his name presents some confusion. Starting in life as Timour, it acquired the addition of 'Leng' – 'the lame Timour' – from a wound he received at the siege of Seistan; as this further developed into Tamerlane it became altogether a more dignified-sounding cognomen for such a ruler than that of 'Timour the Tatar,' as he was not infrequently called. The final inappropriateness of its use was to tack it on to a Scotch reel, certainly stopping short of saying it was his favourite air – but can we picture Tamerlane skipping off his throne to tread such a measure?

It may not be out of place to quote here what Tamerlane says of himself: 'At twelve years of age I fancied I perceived in myself all the signs of greatness and wisdom, and whoever came to visit me I received with great dignity and hauteur. At eighteen' (he does not seem to have possessed much modesty in early life!) 'I became vain of my abilities and was very fond of riding and hunting. I passed much of my time reading the Koran, and playing at chess, and was also very fond of horsemanship.' He seems to have maintained his love for chess, from one incident respecting it. He was engaged in a game when the news of the birth of a son was brought to him, afterwards known as Shah Rokh, from the Persian name of the move, then about to be played, of checking the king with the castle.

With a confidence in himself and his powers he set out at the age of twenty-one on a world-wide conquest, and in thirty years had so far achieved his ambitions that there were few peoples between the Volga and the Ganges that did not own his sway. He was a born leader of men, with a personal magnetism that drew men to him and with a genius for the strategies of war. For instance, on one occasion, finding himself far outnumbered by the enemy, he employed the ruse of dividing his army into seven bodies to give an appearance of greater numbers, and then proceeded to address them in a manner that might have been worthy of the ex-Kaiser: 'This day, brave soldiers, is a day of dancing for warriors, the dancing-room of the heroes is the field of battle; the cries of war are the songs sung and danced to; and the wine which is drunk is the blood of the enemy.'

Tamerlane, with a pride in the job he had set out to accomplish, and not desirous of concealing his soaring projects for earth and heaven, yet with a human touch that appealed to all, thus addressed his troops after one of his many victorious campaigns:

'My heart hath always been set upon enlarging the limits of my vast empire; but now I take up a resolution to use all my care in procuring quiet and security to my subjects, and to render my kingdoms flourishing. I will that private persons address their requests and complaints immediately to myself: I am unwilling that at the day of judgment my poor oppressed subjects should cry out for vengeance against me.

'I am not desirous that any of my brave soldiers, who have so often exposed their lives in my service, should complain against me or fortune; for their afflictions touch me more than they do them. Let none of my subjects fear to come before me with his complaints; for my design is that the world should become a paradise under my reign, knowing that when a prince is just and merciful his kingdom is crowned with blessings and honours. In fine, I desire to lay up a treasure of justice, that my soul may be happy after my death.'

At the conclusion of this speech the whole assembly lifted up their hands to heaven and cried: 'O God, Who art the Lord both of this world and the next, grant us an everlasting reign to this just prince; hearken to his righteous petition, and as Thou hast subjected the universe to him, after a long and prosperous reign in this world, let him reign with Thee in glory in the other.'

Even across the centuries we can still see the glamour of his power and the pride in his empire that he contrived to inspire. As the poet has so powerfully described his ambitious views for a world-domination:

> Tamburlaine, that sturdy Scythian chief,
> That robs your merchants of Persepolis
> Trading by land into the Western Isles,
> And in your confines with his lawless train
> Daily commits incivil outrages,
> Hoping (misled by dreaming prophecies)
> To reign in Asia, and with barbarous arms
> To make himself monarch of the East.
>
> MARLOWE

'On the throne of Samarkand he displayed, in a short repose, his magnificence and power; listened to the complaints of the people; distributed a just measure of rewards and punishments; employed his riches in the architecture of palaces and temples; and gave audience to the ambassadors of Egypt, Arabia, India, Tatary, Russia and Spain, the last of whom presented a suit of tapestry which eclipsed the pencil of the Oriental artists.

'The marriage of six of the Emperor's grandsons was esteemed an act of religion as well as of paternal tenderness; and the pomp of the ancient caliphs was revived in their nuptials. They were celebrated in the gardens of Canighul, decorated with innumerable tents and pavilions, which displayed the luxury of a great city, and the spoils of a victorious camp. Whole forests were cut down to supply fuel for the kitchens; the plain was spread with pyramids of meat and vases of every liquor, to which thousands of guests were courteously invited. The public joy was testified by illuminations and masquerades; the trades of Samarkand passed in review; and every trade was emulous to execute some quaint device, some marvellous pageant, with the materials of their peculiar art.

'After the marriage contracts had been ratified by the cadhis, the bridegrooms and their brides retired to the nuptial chambers; nine times, according to the Asiatic fashion, they were dressed and undressed; at each change of apparel pearls and rubies were showered on their heads, and contemptuously abandoned to their attendants. A general indulgence was proclaimed; every law was relaxed, every pleasure was allowed; the people were free; the sovereign was idle; and the historian of Timour may remark that, after devoting fifty years to the attainment of empire, the only happy period of his life were the two months in which he ceased to exercise his power.

'His spirit of activity would not let him rest; despite his age and infirmities he set out for the conquest of China in the year 1404, and pitched his last camp in the neighbourhood of Otrar, where he was expected by the angel of death. Fatigue, and the indiscreet use of iced water, accelerated the progress of his fever, and the conqueror of Asia expired in the seventieth year of his age' (Gibbon).

'The love and attachment of the army to Timur,' says Wolff, 'was so great and so unlimited that they would forgo plunder in time of need if ordered by him; and the subjection to him was so blind and so unconditional that it would only have cost him an order to cause himself to be proclaimed not only as emperor, but even as Prophet of the Tatars. He endeavoured to soften the inclination to cruelty of his soldiers, composed of so many nations, by poets and learned men, by musicians and *sufis*, who came in swarms to the army and wandered with him through Asia.' The latter were doubtless the equivalent of army chaplains of modern days, and must have been especially favoured by Tamerlane, as it was in his reign that the noted order of dervishes called Nakshabendi was instituted by one of the name of Kawaja Baha-ud-din in 1388. The order is still maintained and is immortalized in a group painted by the famous Russian artist Verestchagin.

The fidelity of his soldiers saw to it that the body of their leader and ruler was embalmed and brought back the long three hundred miles to rest in the tomb he had prepared in his beloved Samarkand.

From various accounts we can picture the closing scenes in this remarkable man's career. Shortly before the end we are told he thus addressed his family and successors to the vast empire he had welded together:

'If you do what my testament directs and make equity and justice the rule of your actions, the kingdoms will remain a long time in your hands; but if discord creeps in among you, ill fortune will attend your undertakings; your enemies will breed war and seditions, which it will be difficult to put a stop to; and irreparable mischiefs will arise both in religion and government.'

For astuteness and foreshadowing of events this speech had few equals.

Tamerlane shortly after expired. He was embalmed and his body wrapt in linen, with camphor, musk and rose-water, and finally placed in an ebony coffin. Before starting on the long return journey evening prayers were said, and the coffin was then covered with velvet and black damask – 'And with it took the road to Samarkand.' At intervals on the way overmastering attacks of grief seemed to seize upon the cavalcade, when 'men cast their turbans upon the ground and flung dust upon their heads, while ladies rent their hair and tore their cheeks with their nails.' Certainly this episode is mentioned as having occurred the morning after they had crossed the Jaxartes on ice, so probably their nerves were a bit upset. As the procession approached Samarkand, Tamerlane's drums and horsehair standard were borne in front and his baggage behind. We can imagine the tragedy of that pageant. Shops and markets were closed, a funeral banquet was served and alms distributed, and then the portal of the Gur Amir was flung open to admit the conquering hero, conquered only by death. Over the grave for the last time his drums were 'beat to a mournful measure.' They were then broken in pieces and the door was closed.

The Citadel, or *urda* (encampment) as it is still called by the people, is one of the outstanding features, both in point of situation and in the history of Samarkand. To it we must go for the first association of Tamerlane as a ruler of the country, for in one of its rooms is still preserved the famous *Koktash*, virtually what is equivalent to our Stone of Destiny in Westminster Abbey. It is in the form of a whitish grey block of polished marble, and there is a carved tracery on each end, while the corners are formed into small pilasters. It measures 10 feet 4 inches long, 4 feet 9 inches wide, and 2 feet high. Part of the coronation ceremony was a formal sitting on this stone, therefore on the occasion of one rebellion a complaint was made that the usurper had never sat upon the *Koktash*, thus showing that his pretensions to the throne were false.

A legend tells that the stone fell from heaven, but that it formed the foundation of Tamerlane's throne seems of less doubtful origin.

Behind it on the wall is an oval memorial tablet inscribed in Coptic characters to a Hodji of the date 1155. A translation tells us that it was erected to 'Sheikh Imam, son of David, son of Ishak of the West. May God bless him, his belongings and all Mussulmans who have died.'

The former audience hall, with carved supporting pillars, may also be seen, and in it there is a curious octagon-shaped stone, slightly hollowed on the top, which was said to have been used for executions.

There is also in the Citadel the subterranean dungeon where prisoners were let down by ropes and in most cases obviated any use being made of the octagon stone above ground. On the stone edge of the hole the marks of these ropes are still visible where they had by long and constant use worn grooves in the stone. Such a barbaric mode of punishment is of ancient origin and is mentioned in the seventh century B.C., when Jeremiah 'was let down with cords into the dungeon of Malchiah that was in the court of the prison; and in the dungeon there was no water, but mire; so Jeremiah sunk in the mire.'

Doubtless it was on the occasion of the return of Tamerlane from the *Koktash* ceremony that he wrote these words: 'When I clothed myself in the robes of empire I shut my eyes to safety and to the repose which is found in the bed of ease'; but on reading his life one cannot but feel that he made it less reposeful than need have been. The present use made of the Citadel is to provide barrack accommodation for the Russian garrison.

Tamerlane's masterly mind soon perceived the need of suitable trade marts, and we are told that 'houses were pulled down which stood in the way of where he desired it to run.' No warning was apparently given to the wretched inhabitants, for 'as the houses came down, their masters fled with their clothes and all they had: then as the houses came down in front, the work went on behind. He covered it with a vaulted roof having windows at intervals to let in the light. Day and night they made such a noise they seemed to be like so many devils.' By dint of relays of workers the structure was finished in twenty days. Some of the owners proposed that compensation should be made to them; there was no surprise expressed at it not being granted, but the only surprise expressed was that they were not killed on the spot for such audacity in suggesting it!

XVII

Tombs & Treasure-Houses

*A Resting-Place – Tamerlane's Ghost – His Nurse
– Shah Zindeh's Tomb – Palace Gardens*

Crossing a slight ravine from the Citadel we come in sight of the
Gur Amir, or tomb of Tamerlane, built by himself in 1386–1404,
and dedicated to his friend and tutor, Mir Sayyid Baraka, who is
buried near the pupil who did him such credit and honour.

Surrounded as it is by trees, chiefly poplar, I can never forget
the sight of that fluted blue dome rising far above the delicate
spring green. On the stone path leading up to the chief portal I
found a little group of natives in gay-coloured *khalats* seated playing chess – a peaceful, undisturbed spot in which to meditate on
their moves – and so absorbed were they in their game that my
presence passed unnoticed.

Over the door of the building is an inscription in Persian stat-
ing that 'the weak slave Mohammed, son of Mahmoud, from
Ispaham, built this.' One is glad to think that the name of such an
artist should be perpetuated as long as his work endures, though
we are told that Tamerlane himself personally superintended the
work, being carried there in a litter, and that slaves from China,
India and Persia were employed as artisans. Apropos of this
Schiltberger tells a tale: 'After Tämerlin was buried, the priests that

belonged to the temple heard him move every night during a whole year. His friends gave large alms, that he should cease his howlings. But this was of no use. They asked advice of their priests, and went to his son and begged that he would set free the prisoners taken by his father in other countries, and especially those that were in Samarkand, who were all craftsmen he had brought to the capital, where they had to work. He let them go, and as soon as they were free, Tämerlin did not howl any more.'

All is now still, but had we ears to hear or power to tap those stones I fear we should find the cries were still entombed. The building is built of brick, made locally, faced with blue tiles in different designs, while the outer fluting of the dome consists entirely of blue tile-work. Where this has been impaired by time or earthquakes the spaces have been filled in with cement.

Around the base of the dome is an inlaid inscription from the Koran: 'There is no God but Allah, and Mahomet is his prophet.' The Arabic letters are of giant size and legible from afar, being traced in white lettering which is outlined by dark blue, and this is thrown up still more clearly by a turquoise tracery pattern on a brick ground. Of the two minarets that flanked the dome only one remains, inlaid in a pattern of coloured tiles.

As we approached, two somewhat sleepy-looking mullahs roused themselves; in mauvy-grey *khalats* and snowy-white turbans they seemed to fit in with the somnolent atmosphere of the place.

As one enters the great portal, or *piktash*, as these arches are called, there is a passage, obscurely lighted, off which open two chambers, in one of which are buried female members of the family of Tamerlane, and in the other his grandson Shah Rokh and his family.

Then comes the vaulted octagon hall, 115 feet in height. Beneath its dome is a white marble railing enclosing seven tombs, the centre one of which is that of Tamerlane, and is of dark green jade, made darker by the contrast of the six others, which are of white marble. This block of jade measures 6 feet in length, 17 inches wide and 14 inches thick. It is the largest known specimen of that stone in existence, although now clasped with an iron clamp across it, and was said to have been the gift of a Mongol princess. Round the edge is an ornamental scroll lettering giving 'Timour's name and titles, together with those of his ancestors and the date of his death 1405.' The light filters in through marble fretted openings, partially illuminating carved and coloured niches alternating with alabaster inscriptions, all relating to Tamerlane's genealogy and heroic deeds. Around the wall for about five feet up is a lining of alabaster hexagon plaques with a eulogistic bordering. In the *mihrab*, or recess, facing Mecca is the standard with horsehair, signifying a militant faith. Beneath this hall is the crypt, where are the actual graves. Near to Tamerlane lies his celebrated astronomer grandson Ulea Beg, who died in 1449, leaving behind him a name for astronomical calculations the accuracy of which is still undisputed.

For beauty of situation and conception of idea the mosques of Shah Zindeh take almost first place among those left by Tamerlane. His scheme of building originated from the sight of a rocky, sandy hillside, with a not unattractive ridge against the sky-line; he there set to work by means of his Persian artists and his Eastern slaves to carry out what his imagination pictured. Up that slope by marbled steps he led his Via Sacra, till the culminating point was reached, and there he erected over the grave of the Shah Zindeh, or 'living saint,' the first of the series of blue-domed tombs with which he crowned the hill. They are seven in all, and beneath them lies a worthy company of family and friends, including two of his sisters and his nurse, called Old-cha Aim.

The tomb of Shah Zindeh is approached through several halls decorated with plaster-work and supporting carved wooden pillars. The tomb itself is in the form of a stone swathed in shawls, visible only through a grating, and still forms a place of pilgrimage, to which in former days the rulers of Samarkand made a special visit before assuming power. Underground cells are even provided for the use of those devotees who may wish to spend the regulation forty days in prayer and fasting.

Many legends circle around Kasim-ibn-Abbas, to give the saint his full name, one being that he suffered martyrdom by decapitation in his efforts to convert the fire-worshipping natives of Samarkand. He picked up his head and jumped down a well which is still shown, from whence he will emerge as the defender of Islam. His failure to appear when the Russians took Samarkand has somewhat shaken his reputation.

Preserved in one of the rooms is a very fine Koran, three feet by two, said to be a sixteenth-century copy of the one belonging to the great reading-stand in the mosque of Bibi Khanum. Through tiled gateways faced with dazzling masses of colour we passed on to recessed tombs whose walls were tiled, and whose ceilings of pendent plaster-work were supported on carved outspreading pillars. Wherever there was any semblance of a wall it was enriched with these wonderful tiles, moulded and embossed, and where more detailed work was required it took the form of mosaic work. Most of the faience was said to have been made in Persia, but one arch was undoubtedly of Chinese origin, and only 'a consummate master of colouring could reproduce the harmony in dark blue, turquoise, yellow and green of this unrivalled panelling.'

Mullahs were in charge of the different tombs, and I was struck by the honesty of the one who was my guide who, after showing me everything on his beat, pointed to a show lamp in charge of the next man, informing him what I had exactly given and that I was not to bestow further largess unless I had some very small coin.

As all these great works of Tamerlane progressed the question of transport must have become a serious one, so he imported ninety elephants from India, which were better able to carry the stones from the quarries, and in even greater quantities than was possible by the long string of camels. To these last was allotted the task of bringing the famous blue tiles all the way from Persia, where they were made. Later on, as art developed, artists and artisans were brought from there and settled in Samarkand, to allow of the work being done nearer at hand; thus gradually a native school of art was founded, based on the Persian with Chinese influence, and to this may be attributed much of the pottery made until recent years in the country.

There is one other bit of mason-work a few miles from Samarkand ascribed to the time of Tamerlane, a gigantic arch strongly built of burnt brick, about one hundred feet in height, with remains of two others, crossing the shallow bed of the Zerafshan, with an apparent fragment of a tower. The use of this has puzzled many savants, but according to Skrine and Ross 'this huge work was built to serve as a regulation of the current, forcing a certain proportion of the water into a channel reserved for the exclusive use of Bokhara, which is entirely at the mercy of Samarkand in the matter of irrigation.' The ruin is called Shadman Malik. According to M. Khainkoff, a bridge over the Zerafshan was known to Arabian geographers under the name of Kantara Samarkand, and was regarded as a marvel. If this be the identical bridge, that places it as one of the oldest ruins in Samarkand. Whatever may have been its use, its present picturesqueness is undeniable.

In coming to the end of those buildings more especially connected with Tamerlane we can better realize how much must have been lost of that of which the following account, written by Clavigo in 1404, gives us some idea: –

'Among these gardens are great and noble houses, and here the lord (*i.e.* Timur) has several palaces. The nobles of the city have their houses amongst those gardens, and they are so extensive that when a man approaches the city he sees nothing but a mass of very high trees. Many streams of water flow through the city and through these gardens, and among these gardens are many cotton plantations and melon grounds, and the melons of this ground are good and plentiful; and at Christmas-time there is a wonderful quantity of melons and grapes.'

From this account we can perceive that Tamerlane's attentions were not confined to the mortar-tub only. Irrigation must have been studied and carried out to enable such high cultivation of the soil and the provision of such luxuries as those mentioned.

With a modern knowledge of the suitable seasons for garden work we are also told: 'In the autumn Tamerlane ordered that at the end of the meadow of Canighul a garden should be laid out, whose beauty should surpass all the gardens which had ever yet been in the Empire.

'The astrologers made choice of the hour in which they were to begin it, and the artists prepared the plans to regulate the alleys, and the compartments of the parterres.

'The painters prepared some new masterpieces to place in the palace which was to be built there; and the most skilful architects of Asia who lived at Samarkand laid the foundations on a square plan, each side of which was fifteen hundred cubits; and in the middle of each was a very high gate.

'The ceilings of the palace were adorned with flowers of all sorts, in mosaic work [which is exactly descriptive of the work of his descendants in their palace at Delhi].

'The walls were covered with porcelain of Cachan. At each of the four corners of the garden a very lofty pavilion was erected, also covered with porcelain, having very delicate shadowings, ranged with admirable art and skill. The parterres of the garden were laid out with perfect symmetry in alleys, square beds, and little wildernesses of divers figures.

'Sycamore-trees were planted on the borders of the alleys; and the compartments on all sides filled with different sorts of fruit trees, and others which only bore flowers.

'When the garden was completed, Timur gave it the name of Baghi Dilencha – that is, "the garden which rejoices the heart."

'In the middle, the foundation of the palace, which was three storeys high, was laid; the roofs were exceeding lofty; it was adorned with all the beauties which could charm the eyes of men; and it was built exceeding strong. It was surrounded with a colonnade of marble, which gave it a majestic aspect.

'As it was customary to dedicate palaces to some lady, Timur dedicated this to his new mistress, Tukel Cannen.'

Tamerlane is said to have been one of the ugliest men in history, and by chance seeing himself one day reflected in a mirror he is said to have been so horrified at the sight that he began to weep. One of his courtiers, in the manner of such men, tried to comfort him by saying: 'If thou hast seen thy face but once, and, seeing, hast not been able to control thy grief, what should we do who look upon thy face every day and every night?' The answer is not recorded.

His dignity and personality were such that all who came within his sphere were, in spite of his personal defects, aware that they were in the presence of no ordinary mortal.

Tamerlane, blind of an eye and lame of a leg, as he hobbled along through life, left marked footprints in history, in spite of those physical disabilities, and worthily earned the title of 'Tamerlane the Magnificent.'

> Still climbing after knowledge infinite,
> And always moving as the restless spheres,
> Wills us to wear ourselves and never rest
> Until we reach the riper fruit of all,
> That perfect bliss and sole felicity,
> The sweet fruition of an earthly crown.

XVIII

Science & Samarkand

*Observatory of Ulea Beg – Daniel's Tomb – Rice Mills – A
Celebrated Koran – A Belated Start – A Night of Horror*

> The compass placed to catch the rising ray,
> The quadrant's shadows studious they survey;
> Along the arch the gradual Index slides,
> While Phoebus down the vertic circle glides.

Three or four miles to the north-east of Samarkand lies the barren
hill of Tchupan-Ata, so called from the shrine of a saint who is
buried on the top. The name means 'Father Shepherd,' and he fills
the dual office of patron saint to the community of shepherds and
to the town of Samarkand, and they do not fail to see that his
tombstone is supplied with the customary offerings of ram's horns:

> I have a fretted brick-work tomb
> Upon a hill on the right hand,
> Hard by a close of apricots,
> Upon the road of Samarkand.

It was on this hill that there once stood the famous observatory built by Ulea Beg, the grandson of Tamerlane, in 1437. All

trace of this building is now lost, but in 1909 the quadrant was discovered, and a quarter of it was then laid bare. It is built of stone with a marble coping upon which are recorded the degrees, in as perfect a condition as the day they were cut, while fragments of the metal rails upon which the instruments were worked are still in place.

I walked down the identical steps – three flights there are, one in the centre of the cutting and one at each side – so often trod by these scientists of that enlightened age. The total radius of the quadrant was said to equal the height of the Mosque of St Sophia. The observatory was originally built to correct the Ptolemaic astronomical tables, to which Ulea Beg added two hundred more fixed stars, and more than a hundred years later Tycho Brahe, the Danish astronomer, found them to be correct.

There is a delightful affinity in that Mahometan part of the world between pilgrimages and picnics, in fact I think it is a special attribute of the East, as witness the perfection to which it is carried in Japan. One such special pilgrimage and pleasuring in Samarkand is to the tomb of Daniel! On a hot day of summer there can be nothing more ideal than such an outing in a wooded ravine, by the banks of the River Zerafshan, and much merit for Heaven must have been gained in this paradise of earth. As to *which* Daniel it is meant to honour there is some confusion; whether it be the prophet Daniel of the Bible, known and venerated by the Sarts, or some Mahometan saint, it is now impossible to determine. The tomb is said to lengthen a few inches every year, and when it has encircled the earth the faith of Islam will dominate the world.

In order to avoid the risk of any such contingency the Russian authorities said this abnormal growth must cease. So Daniel was enclosed with a new wall, inside of which were erected the regulation saints' poles with flags and bunches of horsehair; and a little domed mosque was built over the reputed grave, before which one may see devout visitants absorbed in meditation.

The water of the river at this point is here made use of to establish mills for the husking of rice, and by an ingenious arrangement of cogged wheels the water does the desired work. 'The water turns a rude wheel, from the axle of which project large wooden teeth, if so they may be called; on these teeth lie huge beams, and the wheel goes round these beams, sliding one by one over the ends of the teeth, causing the other end, made like the head of a hammer, to come down with a crash into a mortar, pulverizing the wheat (or rice) which is lying ready there.' This mode of cleaning rice is much preferred by the natives to that done by machinery; probably by experience they find that by the first method the more nutritious parts of the grain are retained.

In the person of Colonel Kastalsky, the engineer commandant of the district, I found one of the few Russians resident in the country who had a real knowledge of the antiquities connected with it. He himself had made an interesting collection of ancient coins found locally, and had also published a pamphlet dealing with the excavation of ancient burials in terra-cotta coffins.

Among his coins was one of the Bactrian period on which was struck the head not alone of the king but of the queen and the heir apparent! The Colonel was employed for three years at Termesse on irrigation work, which involved an expenditure of over £25,000. He also was responsible for the road from Samarkand to Termesse, and the post-houses on it; these he asserted cost 20,000 roubles each, which seemed a large sum for the results attained.

He accompanied me one day to the bazaars, and with a practised eye detected not alone modern frauds but even ancient ones, both in coins and gems. In one shop a dealer was trying to sell things out of a case which was locked, and though four men were in charge of it there was not a key amongst them, so we moved on, and presently the case followed, and with it an augmented crowd, all proffering suggestions. One offered a bunch of the oddest-shaped pieces of metal to be called keys – '*Couleur locale de Samarkand*,' said the Colonel. Another would-be helper offered a pair of tailor's shears! Finally something turned the lock – a bit of piping, I think. 'Thanks be to Allah!' said the Colonel in Arabic, and then proceeded to scoff at all the goods, and shook the falsifications in the faces of the owners.

Samarkand is a great tea depot; 20,000,000 poods (a pood weighs 40 lb.) pass through it for Russia alone annually, apart from what is used in Turkestan. There is also a large trade in brandy made from the native vine products, which is said to be equal to that of France, and is almost entirely exported.

One of the many charms possessed by Samarkand is that of never being able to exhaust so-called 'sights,' and one has always the interest of fresh discoveries, so incomplete is the list of tabulated ones. Shrines and fragments of mosques are either to be met with at unexpected corners or else to be found buried in old gardens. As an early Chinese writer says: 'Even Chinese gardens cannot be compared with them; but the gardens of this country are very quiet: no singing of birds is heard there.' If the singing of birds be not heard in the gardens, one certainly heard it in the open country, where larks abounded. I also have a vivid recollection of nightingales' notes, and in the daytime, not only in twilight hours.

In one such silent garden as the Chinaman describes, I came across the mosque of Hodja Akrar, a noted saint in the Moslem calendar. He lived about four hundred and fifty years ago at Tashkent, and as he early devoted himself to a religious life he joined the order of the Nakshabendi, and ultimately became its head. He was originally named Obeidullah, but was called Akrar (consecrated to God) from his piety. Through his influence the celebrated Koran of Othman (Mahomet's son-in-law) was treasured in this mosque and brought in much revenue from the pilgrims, since they paid for the privilege of kissing and touching it. When the Russians took possession of the country they paid twelve pounds to the authorities for this money-making volume, and removed it to the Imperial Library at Petrograd, where one hopes it may still be preserved. It is a very beautiful specimen, written in Cufic characters on parchment. The tiling of the mosque is fairly perfect, and presents a wonderful collection of designs in blue, orange, and a pale pink colouring, with an even more marked Persian influence in the side panels of the *piktash* than others I had seen, Persian lions crowning the upper surface of the arch, all showing it to be the work of Persian artists. The courts of the once famous college are grass-grown and silent, and there is nothing to disturb the eternal rest of Hodja Akrar in his sycamore grove near at hand.

Wishful to see the birthplace of Tamerlane, Shakr-i-sabz, or 'the verdant city,' I made arrangements one day with a droshky to come the following morning at seven A.M., so as to give sufficient time to reach our destination by evening, a distance of about sixty miles. Seven o'clock struck, eight o'clock, and still no sign of the driver, and when at length he did appear, after repeated summonings, he had no reason to give for this unnecessary delay, which, as events afterwards turned out, just wrecked my plans for seeing Shakr-i-sabz.

> Holla, ye pampered jades of Asia!
> What, can ye draw but twenty miles a day,

And have so proud a chariot at your heels,
And such a coachman as great Tamerlain!

The road out of Samarkand was not worthy of the name. To avoid the deep mud-holes we poised with one side of the carriage on the drier footpath at the imminent risk of being capsized into the quagmire on the other. For miles we proceeded in this manner through cherry orchards then in blossom, but the enjoyment of this was much impaired by the conditions under which we had to travel.

On emerging from the cherry orchards we reached the steppe, which had a much drier surface, and where the road limits were liberal and allowed one to go anywhere, and therefore we did not interfere with the long strings of heavy-coated camels, led as usual by the diminutive donkey. On the steppe a strolling barber had found occupation by the side of a muddy pool on the roadway, into which we splashed, but this did not seem to disturb either him or his two customers!

The first station where we changed horses was on the steppe, where the ground was being cultivated for wheat, and wherever one approached a village the road became much worse. Aman Khutan, where we lunched, consisted of a collection of flat-roofed mud-houses, and scattered among them were *kibitkas*, showing a mixed population. Soon after leaving them behind we began to climb a long hill in a winding ascent of three and a half versts, till the top was reached, where a hurricane was blowing. I deemed it more prudent to get out of the carriage, and walked down most of the way, as the gusts were so frightful and so sudden as to be sufficient to overturn a carriage.

The road is a clever piece of engineering, and round its hairpin turns there is the semblance of a protecting wall. The sides of the mountain are terraced and corn is grown where possible, while the steeper portions are planted with acacia and Spanish chestnut. Six o'clock found us twenty-eight versts from Shakr-i-sabz, at a station called Kaniar, which means 'boiling,' and so named because of some hot springs, and there was no question of proceeding, as several rivers had to be forded and this could only be done by daylight. One was in flood near where we stopped and was therefore impassable. These stations or post-houses are built of stone, or else mud, which is whitewashed, and have a striped black-and-white pole in front to indicate a Government road service. Inside are two rooms, one for natives and the other for Europeans. Luckily on arrival at Kaniar we found both unoccupied. There was no furniture in these rooms except a couple of benches, a table, and one or two chairs. A brass basin was placed on a stand for any who wanted to wash, and a well in the centre of the courtyard supplied sandy water. Of any attempts at sanitary arrangements it was impossible to speak. Half the house had been destroyed by the earthquakes of four years previously and the stones were still left in the roofless rooms, no attempt having been made to clear them away. No food is to be obtained at these post-houses, and with great difficulty I procured a samovar; but with the foresight born of long experience I had brought provisions: indeed the first thing one buys for Central Asian travel is a kettle and a small hamper from which one can always draw supplies.

During the night rain came on, and I never spent a more wretched one. I was roused from a nightmare of being made the target for pea-shooters by drips coming through the ceiling on to me and my bed; the two windows were closely cemented, so there was no ventilation; the horses were lodged next door, so I heard every grind of their teeth as they munched their fodder; mice ran about all over the room and, finally, I was half devoured by fleas, even although I had my own camp-bed. The room was so damp that my gloves were wet and would hardly draw on next morning, and my resolve was then made to return with all speed to a zone of less hardship, as I could not face the possibility of being detained there for days until the floods abated.

By morning the rain was still coming down in sheets, and my heart rather sank at the thought of that awful mountain drive through mist, not to speak of two streams that we had to ford. We could not start until there was some semblance of better weather conditions, which delayed us until nine A.M. We then started, and as soon as we were out of the yard our troubles began, for the mud was indescribable. However, the horses, small as they were, dragged us along until we came to the first ascent, and then they stuck: minus the snow, we were exactly the presentment of an 'old-time Christmas' as pictured on Christmas cards – a shay with a driver half rising from his seat, lashing on the three horses with a short-handled whip and leather thong. All the lashing could not induce the poor beasts to move a yard. Having goloshes, I got out, but as soon as I lifted a foot they were sucked off; then even my shoes suffered a like fate in the mud, which stuck like glue. Replacing them with difficulty, I struggled on minus the goloshes for about half-a-mile, till the worst of the hill was past; but I hope never again to meet with such an experience. When near the top we were able to change our horses for a pair that were stronger.

Fritz's murmured '*Gott sei Dank!*' when we safely crossed the mountain revealed his fear that we never could have achieved it in the mist which had gathered. At the next station where we stopped to change horses the man said we could get them, but after waiting an hour without any appearance of them I told Fritz to ask why they were not coming, and then the postmaster said we could not have them, as they were required for the mail-cart, and that we might have to remain till next day, or the day after – he could not say. Having by this time visited the stable and found six horses in it, I told Fritz to offer the man a rouble, and there was no further difficulty; and this was a Government service with a Government servant!

For the last twelve miles the road was bad beyond words, mud up to the axles, and in one hole I saw the outside horse sink up to its body. How any springed vehicle ever holds together under such conditions is a marvel. And this murderous drive only came to an end in Samarkand at eight P.M.

XIX

Across the Hungry Steppe

An Historic Pass – Desert Stretches – Gay Birds – A Deadly Spider – A Mountain Fort – Singer's Sewing Machines – A College Education

The time had now arrived when farewell had to be said to Samarkand, with all its delights and dreams, its drives and dust, and a move made eastward to Andijan, the terminus of the Transcaspian Railway.

I stopped at various places *en route*, but as a rule there was little to remind one of past history, and the uneventful present was only in the making.

Soon after leaving Samarkand, with its fertile suburbs and fruitful orchards, one enters a section of desert country which swells into the low hills of the Pass of Jilanuti, so named from its serpentine windings, or, as the natives explain its meaning, 'a serpent has passed.' In no place does it exceed a hundred yards in breadth, and but for the warlike memories it arouses would call for little notice. It was the scene of many fierce struggles between Mongol and Turkish hordes, both striving to reach the coveted valley of the Zerafshan. Two of these battles are commemorated in Persian inscriptions cut upon the face of one of the two higher rocks which are called the 'Gates of Tamerlane,' though without any historical reason for the name, except the family connection of his grandson, Ulea Beg, who caused his victory to be thus perpetuated in the following words:

> With the help of God the Lord, the great Sultan, conqueror of kings and nations, shadow of God on earth, the support of the decisions of the *Sunna* and of the divine law, the ruler and aid of the faith, Ulea Beg, Gurugan (may God prolong the time of his reign and rule!), undertook a campaign in the country of the Mongols, and returned from this nation into these countries uninjured, in the year 828 (A.D. 1425).

The second inscription of Abdullah, Khan of Bokhara, in 1571, is much more bloodthirsty, and records that he slew four hundred thousand of the enemy, till rivers ran blood.

After passing the station of Jizakh comes the desert called by the Russians 'Golodnaya,' or 'hungry steppe,' and little seems to have been done in the course of centuries to cause it to merit any other designation. The Chinese traveller Hiouen Thsang in A.D. 629 thus describes his experience of it:

> One enters into a great sandy desert, where neither water nor grass is to be found. It is necessary to look at some high mountain in the distance, and seek for abandoned bones, to know how to guide oneself and recognize the path to be followed.

Thanks to the railway one is now carried across in a much more comfortable manner, without the gruesome task of having to look for abandoned bones! The junction of Tchernaievo was my objective preparatory to driving to Ura Tiubbe. This town was founded by Cyrus I., King of Persia, in 550 B.C., and named Cyropolis after him. It was the most easterly town of the Persian Empire. Having secured the only droshky the station offered, I set off at six P.M. across part of the 'hungry steppe.' It is an absolute desert, with the exception of some scrubby-looking plants, such as thyme, or another with peony-like leaves and hemlock-looking flowers rising out of their clusters. The leaves apparently were used as fodder for some animal, as they were being cut and carried off by the natives on the backs of camels.

I never anywhere saw such numbers of tame larks hopping about quite fearlessly, even close to the horses' feet. Goldfinches, too, were nearly as common as sparrows at home, and many other gay-plumaged birds, one a blue crow – at least, a crow I felt sure he must be, though I am no ornithologist. Fear of less pleasant inhabitants of the steppe kept me pinned to the carriage. One of the most deadly of all insects is a black spider called *Kara-kourt*. I never saw it nearer than safely drowned in a bottle of spirits of wine. Its body is a little larger than a bee and it looks harmless enough, but so venomous is the poison of its sting that a camel is dead in three hours after being stung, and a human being in less time. The sheep which feed on the scanty herbage of the steppe do not apparently suffer from its presence.

After forty versts of this country cultivation began, and the background of hills became more impressive as Ura Tiubbe drew near. The snow-capped peaks of the Turkestan and Zerafshan mountains towered aloft, one to the south-east, called Abdu-Baisher, even reaching 20,000 feet. Regarding it the natives have the following legend.

A wealthy Tadjik, a native of Hodjent, had a large family who all died young. At length a son was born to him, and the mother, fearful that he too might be taken from them, consulted a witch as to the fate of the child. She was told that all would be well until he reached the age of sixteen, when he would die from the bite of one of those terribly fatal black spiders. The father to counteract such a fate took the child in his cradle to the summit of Abdu-Baisher, where no scorpions, spiders, or serpents could abide. The child throve, and to celebrate his sixteenth birthday his parents decided to give a feast. Apparently such a climb was nothing to the guests, and when all had assembled the boy gave a cry, fell down, and died. Among the fruits provided for the feast was a basket of grapes, in which the attendants found the black spider that had spun the thread of fate predicted by the witch. The youth was buried in his mountain home, and a cloud of snow fell and covered him and his parents, but in remembrance of them the sun sheds its golden rays once a day upon the mountain-top.

The pronunciation of Ura Tiubbe varies but little, but its diversity of spelling becomes almost a joke. After the decline of the Persian Empire it was known as Oshrusene, Osrushene and Satrushene; how this developed into Ura Tiubbe, Uratepe, Ura-Tippe and even Ora-Tippa would be hard to explain. Not less varied were the masters by whom it was ruled, always, however, bursting out now and again into an independent administration of its own.

In succession, its allegiance was claimed by Khokand, Tashkent, Khodjend, and Bokhara, and it was only on the fall of the latter province in 1866, when the domination of Russia was assured, that Ura Tiubbe fell under the government of the province of Ferghana.

After a fierce resistance under its late Beg, Abdul Gaffar, when the Citadel was besieged for eight days by General Romanovski, it was finally taken by assault, the Russian guns proving too formidable for the less efficient weapons pitted against them. Only the courage born of a mountain people inured to raids and broils and family feuds enabled them to withstand for so long a time the superior forces brought against them.

Picturesquely situated on a mountain slope, the ruins of its fort first meet the eye, with towers and remains of the old wall on one hill, and the ruined fragments of the fortress on the other, like two guardian bulwarks. A narrow stream serves to water the numerous gardens and trees that are scattered among the flat-roofed mud-houses of a fairly large town; it is dammed in places, and rivulets are run from it, so a pleasing diversity is formed, as houses are built overhanging the banks. Altogether Ura Tiubbe is a most attractive spot, and I deeply regretted not having longer time to spend in it – unfortunately, as was always the case with places at all off the beaten track, no one could give any information either as to its interest or possible accommodation, so I visited it only on chance, guided by the instinct that had so often served me in the past under similar circumstances.

Certainly Ura Tiubbe did not offer luxuries, but the station-house for changing horses was quite clean, with low brick platforms used as beds, upon which one was expected to spread felt rugs and pillows to mitigate the hardness of such a couch. They were not unlike those met with in China, heated by a stove beneath, but minus the warming arrangement.

The winding streets of the bazaars were enticing to linger in, with commodities suited for mountain customers, such as green riding-boots studded with silver nails, and wooden three-legged clogs into which spikes were driven to give a better foothold on precipitous paths.

While strolling around a pleasant-faced native came up with a smile of recognition and shook me warmly by the hand.

Curious to know who my unknown friend could be, by means of the Interpreter I asked when I had had the pleasure of seeing him last, and was told that he had seen me in the bazaars of Bokhara, an encounter which was evidently quite looked upon as a basis of friendship in such a remote region. I was then informed that he was the agent at Ura Tiubbe for 'Singersky' – *i.e.* Singer's sewing machines! He was riding a nice little chestnut pony, so I photographed them both, much to his delight, and afterwards sent him a copy. His action in thus greeting me was significant of the general friendliness I found amongst the natives of Ura Tiubbe.

Of the older buildings the principal mosque is the most interesting, with its Persian tile façade of turquoise-blue; from their colour I should say it was fourteenth-century work, and as usual when of that period the emblems of the lion and the sun are inserted above the portal. In out-of-the-way corners one finds old buildings, insignificant perhaps as to size, but one with carved slender pillars supporting a veranda and another with painted Persian decoration – all demanding more time than I could spare to study them. Among more modern buildings is the college of Rustam Beg, built about 1840, in imitation of the Shir-dar at Samarkand, and from its commanding situation it is an outstanding feature in any view of the town.

In addition to a close study of the Koran, calligraphy forms a not unimportant part of the curriculum of a *medresse*, but in order to gain distinction a high standard is claimed from the students. It may not be out of place to give here a sample of the copy-book maxims by which the youths are doubly instructed:

'Select thy friends from among the capable and the intelligent.'

'Avoid stupid and ignorant men.'

'Place not thy confidence in women, even if they appear to be trustworthy.'

'Prove thy words by thy actions.'

'Seek to learn of men who are successful in life.'

'Regulate thy expenses according to thy income.'

'Always avoid extremes.'

'Treat in a becoming manner the guests thou hast invited.'

'Is it not known that everything which falls among salt changes itself to salt after a certain length of time? If then thou art desirous that thy name should resound from the sky above to the uttermost bounds of the earth, take a vow that thou wilt enter the service of eminent men, be it only for a few days of thy life.'

I have quoted these sayings as showing the amount of worldly wisdom and shrewd sagacity inculcated by the early teachers, as they are sayings that have been handed down and taught to generation after generation of students at a period of history when education in our own country was of a very elementary kind indeed.

It is such touches that make one realize the advanced civilization which was the possession of that part of Central Asia in those remote days.

XX

Khokand or Cottonpolis

*A Cotton Mart – Troublous Times – The Emir's
Palace – Hair Tassels – Native Jewellery –
Aldershot Ovens – Fruit Cultivation*

Leaving the 'hungry steppe' near the town of Khodjend, we speedily – if the word 'speed' can be applied to a Central Asian train,
whose average is seventeen miles an hour – reach the confines of
the fertile province of Ferghana. Surrounded by snow-covered
peaks and watered by the Syr Daria (so named after the junction
of the two rivers Naryn and Kara Daria at Namangan), it has been
one of the most coveted spots of earth in Central Asia, in ancient
as well as modern days. It is now the garden of Turkestan and the
chief district for cotton-growing. In the desire for possession its
surface has been drenched with blood again and again, while
deeds of cruelty and wholesale slaughterings stain the pages of its
history.

As one of the three great Khanates – Bokhara, Khiva, and
Khokand forming the triumvirate – it was the last to surrender to
Russia, but as soon as the other two had capitulated it was only a
question of time when the Emir would be forced to resign grace-
fully the independence of his Khanate. Let us see what happened
in earlier times, although of any clear history there is very little

that is authentic. Khokand was one of the provinces given by Ginghiz Khan to his son Jagatai. Baber mentions it as belonging in his day to the dominion of Samarkand, and gives a record of feuds and victories, by which the sovereignty of the country was tossed like a shuttlecock from one prince to another, till at the beginning of 1800 it emerged as an independent state.

Alim Khan, who was then the ruler, was the first to style himself Khan: he ordered his name to be recited in the daily prayers at the mosque; he struck a coinage made out of the old bronze cannon left by Nadir Shah, and plated it with silver – quite a handsome inauguration to his reign! Being murdered in 1812, his brother Omar succeeded him; he in turn was poisoned by his elder son, Mahmoud, afterwards known as Mohammed Ali, or Medalim Khan. No more poisonings are for a time recorded, but Mohammed Ali promptly exiled most of his relatives. He concluded a favourable treaty with the Chinese, and altogether had the reputation of a good sovereign. But suddenly a change came over him and he embarked on a licentious career, was over-powered by the Khanate of Bokhara, and finally executed by the orders of its council. Disorder upon disorder took place, accompanied on one occasion by a wholesale massacre of 20,000 men. The Russians were determined to end this, and after still further slaughtering and ravaging, the country was formally annexed by the Tsar. This annexation was announced in a euphonious address made to the inhabitants, that their prayer to become Russian subjects had graciously been heard and granted! Khokand was to be known in future as part of the district of Ferghana, and was placed under the rule of General Skobelof, who had already gained his laurels in the conquest of that quarter of Turkestan.

According to Schuyler, 'the exactions of Khudayer Khan were one of the causes of the discontent of the population, which broke out into so many rebellions.' The chief complaints were that 'to keep the roads in repair, to build houses for the Khan, to cultivate his gardens and to clear out the canals men are seized in all parts of the country and forced to work. These get no pay, not even their food; and besides this, when half a village is forced to work, the other half is compelled to pay a tax of two *tengas* (11d.) a day for each man during his work. Anyone who runs away or who refuses to pay is whipped. Sometimes people have been whipped to death, and others have been buried alive in the place of work. This same forced labour existed under previous Khans, but with less cruelty, and the workmen at least received their daily food.' With the advent of the Russians this system of *corvée* was in a great measure abolished, and the workman was considered worthy of his hire.

The management of the irrigation department is in the hands of a native official called *Aryk-Aksakal*, who settles disputes as to supply and demand, sees that canals are kept open, and though not above accepting a bribe from some farmer who may be specially anxious as to his crops, sees to it in a general way that there is a fair distribution of water.

Khokand, a town of about 90,000 inhabitants, is the second in importance of Russian Asiatic possessions and the capital of the province of Ferghana. It is a wealthy city, and is the centre of the cotton industry, which year by year has steadily increased, until in 1912 its trade reached a total of 11,000,000 poods (a pood is about 40 lb.), and Russia was thus well within sight of being entirely self-supporting in this commodity. All this has grown from what was apparently a very insignificant beginning.

I had the pleasure of meeting in Petrograd a Frenchman, M. Gourdet by name, whose educational interests took him in the sixties to Turkestan. In 1869 he was residing in Tashkent, and a friend in America sent him fifty seeds of American cotton to try if they would grow in his garden. He sowed them and they did grow, and the following year he sowed more, and from that experiment of those fifty seeds was evolved the riches of Ferghana and its capital, Khokand.

There are many wealthy inhabitants, it is said to the number of 100,000, Russian, Jewish and native, who live extravagantly, and who are said to consume the most expensive brands of champagne that France can produce, for as usual in these remote Russian possessions dancing, drinking and gambling are the only amusements provided for. There is an exchange, and this causes fluctuating fortunes in cotton gambling. Rents are very high, so that on account of this there is less demarcation between the Russian and the native towns. In point of distance they are not far apart, and so the less wealthy families are obliged to live in a locality that better suits their purse, while the more opulent, whether Russian or native, live in the newer and more pretentious abodes.

All this trade and commerce centred in Khokand was contrary to the plan originally proposed by the Russians, which was to make New Mergilan, afterwards called Skobelof, the capital of the province, both from its being more conveniently situated, and also because of the unhealthiness of Khokand; but in the latter there was capital and a commercial spirit, both of which are difficult suddenly to create. The unhealthiness was very apparent to even a casual visitor like myself. I never remember having seen in any place so many sufferers from goitre, attributed to the unwholesomeness of the water, and little was done to counteract the disease – indeed rather the reverse, to judge from an incident I saw. Along a roadside ditch I watched a strolling refreshment-seller. He had an earthenware pot in which he had large lumps of ice which he churned up with milk; when a customer came along he gave two pieces of ice in a bowl with the milk, and after the thirsty one had drunk the liquid the bits were put back in the pot, while another pot was kept cool in the filthy ditch by which he had ensconced himself.

As regards public buildings, the most interesting is the palace of the late Emir, now used as barracks. There is a fine façade all faced with white, blue, green and yellow tiles, with towers at the two corners and also at each side of the great doorway, which is approached by a wide sloping pavement. The tiles are inlaid in vertical and diagonal designs, and the frontage is relieved by arched recesses, also inlaid. Along the top in large lettering is the inscription: 'Built by Seid Mohammed Khudayar Khan in the year 1287' (Mahometan reckoning). There is also in connection with the late ruling family of Emirs their burying ground, walled round with an ornamental coping and towers at the corners, while the tombstones are kept in tolerable repair within the enclosure.

The bazaars of Khokand are better built on the whole than in some towns of Central Asia, but one should visit them first, before seeing those of Bokhara, which spoil one for any others. There is one collection of stalls devoted to a rather unique form of female adornment – namely, hair tassels. The hair is done up in countless little plaits, and when it reaches the waist-line, or sooner, should nature demand it, wool or silk is then introduced to increase the length, when the silk attached to the tassels is then added. There is an endless variety of them. The more expensive ones are made in silver-gilt and inlaid with small turquoises; or a species of papier mâché is used, gilt over, and weighted. Then there are plain silver tops, which are threaded with coral beads, bits of glass or stones, anything to make a gay appearance, and all these oddments have brightly coloured silk knots and braids, and sometimes a broad band of silk netting in bright crimson is mixed among them.

One very distinctive form of jewellery is that of the crushed turquoise cloisonné work, similar to that made in Kashmir, but of better quality, as the stones are set in silver; it is made into buttons, buckles, sword ornaments, and European ornaments.

Paper-making has been an industry for long, owing to the suitability of the water for the purpose and the supply of rice straw at hand, but now it seems rather on the decline, as where printing is introduced an inferior quality of material can be employed.

In exploring the bazaars I found a tiny shop, the owner of which was a genuine lover of less perishable goods; some were for sale and others not, as he collected for the real pleasure of it. I could have wished that his affections had not been so centred on an enviable steel dog inlaid with gold and silver, of old Persian work, which I would gladly have called my own.

In the food-selling quarter I was particularly interested to find what must have been the origin of the cooking arrangement known as the 'Aldershot oven.' On the high raised platform of a shop front I saw a row of what seemed to be Ali Baba oil-jars made of pottery, fired but unglazed. Each has a hole at one side and one on the top; through the side opening is thrust dried grass and twigs, which is set alight, and when all is consumed the ashes are swept out, and at once the inner sides are plastered with little loaves, or meat cakes, the under-side having been wet to make them stick. Both apertures are then closed by clods of earth until the necessary time has elapsed for the cooking of the food. An effective method and very economical as to fuel.

Considering the affluence of the town the streets were in a lamentable condition, unpaved in any fashion, and after rain one day in the principal street there were ponds of water which had to be planked across, or navigated by the high wheels of the *arbas*.

One bright spot of life in a rather indifferent hotel was the memory of the sweet scent of acacia blossoms blowing in at my window and the installation of a bath with hot and cold water. It is true that timely notice had to be given that hot water would be required, and an hour stated, as it was a matter of some time to get all the preparations made, and then holidays had to be reckoned with in the choice of selecting a day and an hour. Oh no, the order for a bath cannot be lightly or unadvisedly taken in Khokand.

Ferghana aspires also to taller specimens of vegetation than the humble-growing cotton. Its walnuts are famed, its mulberries not less so, though the tree is chiefly cultivated for the sake of its leaves, with which to feed the silkworms that are reared in considerable numbers by the natives, the cocoons being an article of commerce, and also used to supply the silk mills of Khodjent. The orchards are prolific, and the Lombardy poplar may almost be described as growing in forests, while I frequently saw an attractive black-stemmed willow with silvery white leaves shading the tea-drinkers of the *tchai khans*.

A branch line of the railway goes to Mergilan, a two and a half hours' journey owing to a long detention at a junction. New Mergilan, now called Skobelof, is a very beautifully laid-out town, with wide avenues of trees, and rippling water between the double rows of poplars, willows, and yellow acacia, which in spring scented the air with its blossom. The houses are usually of one storey on account of earthquakes, with their woodwork, inside and out, painted a light grey. This is almost the universal colour of the country for inside painting of doors and windows.

Old Mergilan, which claims to have been once the home of Iskander Macedonsky, the Russian name of Alexander the Great, is about ten miles distant, and is said to have received its name from the following incident. Alexander the Great in his march of conquest from India approached Mergilan, but his reputation had preceded him, and the inhabitants, fearful of losing all they possessed, resolved to see what propitiation could do, so they sent a deputation with a hen and a loaf of bread, which are the Sart emblems of hospitality. This so pleased Alexander that he resolved to take the town under his protection, and renamed it Margihan, which means 'bread-hen.' I fear that this is but a legend, for in the old writings the place was called Marghinan, but possibly that resembles Margi-han as much as Mergilan!

Baber in his *Memoirs* gives this description: 'Another district is Marginan, which lies on the west of Andijan. It is noted for its pomegranates and apricots. There is one species of pomegranate, named *dana-kalian* (or great seed), which, in its flavour, unites the sweet with a sweet acid, and may even be deemed to excel the pomegranate of Semnan. They have a way of taking out the stone of the apricot and of putting an almond in its place, after which the fruit is dried. When so prepared it is termed *seikhani*, and is very pleasant. The game and venison are also excellent. All the inhabitants are Sarts; the men are great boxers, noisy and turbulent; so that they are famous all over Maverannahr for their blustering and fondness for boxing.'

In 1820 Nazarof says: 'The bazaar is built of several rows of shops, and on two days of the week is crowded from morning to evening. In this town they manufacture various kinds of goods, among others Persian cloth of gold, velvet, and various Asiatic stuffs, which they send to Bokhara and Kashgar. From this latter place they receive tea, porcelain, ingots of silver, dyes, and all the best Chinese wares. The inhabitants lead a comfortable and tranquil life.'

For a rather more modern description we must go to Schuyler, who says: 'Marghilan, which contains about 30,000 inhabitants, is surrounded by a high wall, and in almost every street are pretty little *mazars*, or chapels, built in the Persian style with bulbous domes, mosaic fronts, and much alabaster fretwork. These give to the town a bright and cheerful air. The streets of the bazaar are chiefly covered over as at Khokand, and the bazaar is full of fearful smells.'

It is wonderful how comparatively little change there is in these Asiatic towns, in the general description by those writers; most of it is applicable to the present day, and not least true is that statement of the atmosphere of the bazaars! All the country around reminds one very much of North Italy, including a very similar agriculture, and means of irrigation, with a background of the snow-clad Alai Mountains. On those slow railway journeys one had ample time for observation. I left Mergilan at two P.M. and did not reach Andijan until six P.M., a distance of under fifty miles! Every station along the route offered scenes of interest from the many and varied races congregated at each one, but chief among them were:

> The Tatars of Ferghana, from the banks
> Of the Jaxartes, men with scanty beards
> And close-set skull-caps.

XXI

Andijan & Ush

Death of King Edward – Grapes and Gardens – Good-Natured Crowds – A Wonder Storm – Practical Jokes

> Far in the south I know a land divine,
> And there is many a saint and many a shrine,
> And over all the shrines the blossom blows
> Of roses that were dear to you as wine.

Andijan is the terminus of the Transcaspian Railway and the starting-point for the Pamirs and Kashgar. As a town it offers little attraction, most of it having been destroyed by the earthquakes of 1902, but there is still sufficient left of it to accommodate a population of about 70,000 inhabitants, and what has been rebuilt of the houses are all on the safer plan of one storey. Even the bazaars have a shaken look about their light wood roof frames, upon which mats are hung to provide shade.

The morning after my arrival I was wakened by shrieks of all kinds of poultry in the courtyard of the hotel; the daily slaughter was taking place, but at least at that hour the corpses would have time to get cold before being presented at table. On two occasions I found the birds or animals had been killed while I was waiting for lunch, and the result was a most stringy disgusting mess.

On going to the bank, the morning after my arrival, the manager engaged the Interpreter in conversation, when the latter suddenly dissolved into floods of tears. I asked, 'What has happened?' and between his sobs he ejaculated: 'The king is dead.' Not knowing who his king was, I again had to ask: 'What king?' And after further delay, while he pulled himself together, he said: 'The King of England.' News had just come by wire that his Majesty had died three days before, but the banker added that it was a rumour and not yet confirmed. However, after a fortnight the sad news was verified and the Interpreter had not shed his tears in vain. The attitude of the Russian Press was one expressive of his loss to the world. And even among the natives all spoke regretfully of his decease, and how much respect they had for him – a great testimony that his influence was so widely spread in such a distant land.

Of Andijan Baber says: 'It abounds in grain and fruits, its grapes and melons are excellent and plentiful. There are no better pears produced than those of Andijan. The district abounds in birds and beasts of game. Its pheasants are so fat that the report goes that four persons may dine on the broth of one of them and not be able to finish it. The inhabitants are remarkable for their beauty. Hodja Yusuf, so famous for his science in music, was a native of Andijan. The air is unwholesome, and in the autumn agues are prevalent.'

A droshky having been secured for next morning, I started the thirty miles' drive to Ush, on the way to Kashgar. For about twenty miles we drove through an avenue of acacia-trees, then in full flower, which filled the air with their sweet scent. Half-way we changed horses. The land is well cultivated, with villages at inter-vals, and, except actual beggars, everyone rides on horseback; so horses must be cheap, or money plentiful, though the beasts were rather a poor type of breed, with sloping quarters.

I feel sure the natives in choosing either their *khalats* or steeds do so with an eye to suitable combinations. For instance, the wearer of a dark blue *khalat* would ride a chestnut pony; mulberry-colour or shades of orange and green would be mounted on a white horse; some riders wore turbans or else embroidered caps, and reminiscent of Tibetan lands was the white felt hat turned up with black velvet – a very becoming headgear. The children are exceedingly pretty, with lovely complexions, the boys dressed in *khalats* like their fathers, while the little girls wear a long loose brightly coloured cotton garment, trousers to the ankles, their hair done up in dozens of plaits, with a gay handkerchief tied round their head. They are most attractive, bright little people. The women as usual have the hideous square of black horsehair covering their faces, and are enveloped in a dark coloured garment.

The town of Ush is built on a tributary of the Syr Daria, and has interesting bazaars, but of course no tourists; strangers of any kind are rarely met with. I was quite mobbed by an orderly crowd till at last a species of street scavenger took me under his protection, and with his very long-handled spade shovelled the people off when approaching too near, so I took a photograph of him and his good-humoured crowd, much to their amusement. My eye having caught sight of a lovely little panther cub skin hanging up, I bought it for two shillings, and after that catskins were brought for sale from every recess of the bazaar in hope of a deal.

Beside the native town rises a rock called Tahkt-i-Suleiman (the Hill of Solomon), a place of pilgrimage, and said to be the spot where Solomon established his throne to survey that part of the world. More probably some confusion has arisen with a local saint of the same name, but the virtue of the pilgrimage is not thereby impaired in the minds of those undertaking it. The climate of Ush is a healthy one, and so this makes it quite a summer resort for visitors both from Kashgar and from the lower situated towns of Ferghana. The Russian quarter has its houses of a simple kind buried in gardens which must be delightfully cool in summer. Along the river bank are tea-houses with covered balconies overhanging the water, and there is a bridge across the river uniting both parts of the town.

The day I spent at Ush had the additional excitement of the sitting of an assize court which meets there only once in six months and comes from Tashkent. A local court was also having a pow-wow in a café, all the men seated on the ground, while their horses, tied to trees, patiently awaited their masters. I left on the return journey at four P.M., and by five P.M. had the most glorious view of the mountains, the higher peaks of the Pamirs tinged pink in the setting sun. On the opposite side of the sky was a heavy bank of grey cloud across which flashed rosy sheet-lightning and forked silver of a blinding sort. The air seemed almost to flicker with electricity, while the flashes never ceased, and after a time it made one's eyes almost ache with the side-glances of light that one could not avoid seeing. There was no thunder, and luckily the horses did not seem to mind the lightning. We had no lamps and were literally flashed home by nine P.M., after again changing horses half-way. I was not sorry to find myself under a roof once more, in spite of such a wonder storm.

Baber gives a very interesting account of Ush as it appeared in his day, and it is so applicable to the present, after a lapse of more than four hundred years, that I venture to give it: 'The air of Ush is excellent. It is abundantly supplied with running water, and is extremely pleasant in spring. On the south-east of the fort is a mountain of a beautiful figure, named Bara-Koh, on the top of which Sultan Mahmud Khan built a small summer-house, beneath which, on the shoulder of the hill, I built a larger palace and colonnade (A.D. 1496).

'The whole town with its suburbs lies stretched out below. The river of Andijan, after passing through the outskirts of Ush, flows on towards Andijan. On both of its banks there are gardens, all of which overlook the river. Its violets are particularly fragrant. It abounds in streams of running water. In the spring its tulips and roses blow in great profusion. On the skirt of this same hill of Bara-Koh, between the hill and the town, there is a mosque, called the Mosque of Juza; and from the hill there comes a great and wide stream of water. Beneath the outer court of the mosque there is a meadow of clover, sheltered and pleasant, where every traveller and passenger loves to rest. It is a standing joke among the common people at Ush to let out the water from the stream upon all such as fall asleep there.'

I like the idea of the practical jokes being played upon the pilgrims, it gives such a very human touch to the description, and an insight into the character of the people. As Goethe says: 'Nothing shows the character more of a people than in what things they find humour.'

XXII

The Journey from Petrograd to Tashkent

Preparations for a Journey – Lack of Luxury – Hand Luggage – Volga Bridge – General Sukhomlinoff – Wayside Inspections – Royal Reception

I shall not weary the reader with an account of how I made my journey home from Andijan: suffice it to say that after five days of dusty travel by the Tashkent-Orenburg Railway, unbroken by any incidents worthy of note, I found myself at Moscow, and there, while revelling in the comfort of its excellent hotel, I made up my mind that if possible I would return to Central Asia.

The memory of the delights of travel there did draw me again, and on this occasion I decided to repeat the journey via Petrograd-Moscow-Tashkent Railway, which is usually performed in a space of time not exceeding five days, and under conditions which are fairly comfortable, the chief unpleasantness being the intense heat and stuffiness of the carriages, which have little or no ventilation. It is impossible to open the double-sealed windows, and even were one to succeed I doubt whether the conditions would be much improved, because of the dust that would threaten to stifle anyone bold enough to try.

Having arrived from England in Petrograd, my stay there was unduly prolonged: first, because of delay in obtaining the necessary permit to go to Central Asia, and, secondly, because of the extreme difficulty of finding any man who would go to these far-off regions in the capacity of interpreter and servant. Eventually, after many applications, he was discovered in the person of Fritz, who has already figured in these pages and who was always ready for any adventures that might befall. I had the offer of all kinds, men and women, suitable and unsuitable, but among all the applicants not one had ever before travelled in the country; but all said they wished to go there, and each seemed to think him and her self fit to undertake the journey.

Among various cards handed to me was one which bore the following inscription: – 'Professeur de la littérature à l'école des langues étrangères à Tokio, dragoman de la direction du chemin de fer chinois de l'est, attaché au Ministère de Finance, secrétaire de la Société des Orientalistes Russes.' I did not see him blacking boots, brushing clothes, or cooking if need be, and had I taken him no one card could have contained further honours. I felt if I delayed much longer my courage would gradually ooze away, so many were the dangers and difficulties presented by kindly interested friends, who all seemed to regard the journey as bristling with terrifying possibilities.

Fritz was warned to take firearms, which mercifully he did not, as real troubles would probably then have begun, while my own friends, after enumerating a list of likely ills, summed up, 'and you will have no one to talk to.' I replied: 'I have books.' 'But what is that!'

The journey, which had as its ultimate object a second visit to Bokhara and Samarkand, was enlivened by the presence of the then Minister of War, General Sukhomlinoff, travelling on a tour of inspection, and in full state as the representative of the Tsar to his remote dominions. Such an illustrious passenger added materially to the difficulty of arrangements for those of less note, but this was almost compensated for in the interest of the State ceremonies that took place at every station at which we stopped.

Each train is made up of only a certain number of carriages, no matter how few or many those requiring them may be. Tickets are sold in the town at certain offices, as well as at the station itself, and apparently by some strange arrangement only one-third of them are to be obtained at the booking office, opened one hour before the train starts. The fares are not exorbitant, and are calculated in zones, so the farther the journey the cheaper it becomes. From Petrograd to Tashkent, a distance of 3000 miles, the second-class ticket costs only about four pounds.

By four P.M. a queue of would-be passengers had formed for the train which left at eight-thirty P.M., and in addition to this inconvenience a couple of roubles had to be slipped into the expectant palm of the booking clerk in order to procure a seat at all. This I found in a second-class compartment, the only first available for the public being half a carriage, already booked, all else being taken up by the Minister of War and his staff.

My compartment was shared by two Russian women; one, the wife of a doctor, was going to Petrovsk, and the other to Moscow. They at once fell to chattering; the only fragment of which I could grasp was a half whisper that I was French!

The whole of the luggage belonging to the doctor's lady was with her. An enormous round hat-box that threatened to annihilate the unlucky passenger on whom it fell was removed, but there were still left one bundle, and two boxes of huge proportions, besides odds and ends of parcels, a bunch of willow in view of the approaching Palm Sunday, and a large, very large, blue enamel tea-kettle.

Subsequently these bundles produced all the comforts and most of the food required for the next five days. At every station out popped the tea-kettle to be filled with the necessary hot water; six tea leaves were extracted from a tiny packet, dropped into a midget teapot, and the water added; after a few minutes a spoonful of this liquid was put into a tumbler, and this again was filled up from the tea-kettle. What I made for myself and drank, though far from strong, was called *bortsch* by my fellow-traveller, who no doubt regarded it much as we do the famous churned tea of Tibet. The lady's husband came in at frequent intervals to air his German and enlarge upon all the possible diseases of Turkestan.

Our company was increased of an evening by a Colonel Viartzin, resident in Turkestan for forty years, and with a great knowledge of the country and its people, some of which he obligingly communicated. Though then retired, he still wore uniform, as a reward for special services – a reward which I fear British officers in similar circumstances would hardly regard as a prized privilege.

For hundreds of miles we travelled over vast snow-fields, with forests of birch-trees, whose shining white tree trunks stood out against the snows, cold and bleak. After crossing the Ural river the desert shortly appeared, the snow vanished gradually and the dust began, and before reaching Tashkent a perceptible warmth was felt in the sunshine.

At Batraki, on the Volga, a rush was made by the female passengers to purchase *sterlets*, a species of small sturgeon, and esteemed a delicacy, the men apparently looking forward to sharing in the joys of this smoked relish. My travelling companion pressed a prime cut upon me, but my politeness could not extend to consuming this raw dainty.

At a short distance from Batraki a bridge one and a quarter versts (about a mile) long crosses the Volga. The building of it was begun in 1876 and finished in 1880, when it was named the Alexander Bridge, after the Tsar. Before the train left the river bank two old ladies lighted candles and began to pray fervently for a safe passage, and continued to do so till the other side was reached, which we did in six minutes. The shadow of this long bridge with its thirteen arches reflected by moonlight on the ice of the river was a striking sight.

On seeing that magnificent River Volga for the first time one can quite realize all the feelings of pride and affection that are lavished upon it by the Russian people. 'Matushka,' or little mother, as they fondly name it, is worthy of all the praise that has been poured out on it in song and story, and as we glided from its banks the haunting refrain of the Volga boat-song rendered on the balalaika by some traveller long remained a memory.

Owing to the presence of our distinguished passenger the day's incidents were not lacking in variety. He was a man with an imposing presence, and carried out the part allotted to him with becoming dignity. Who could have foreseen another drama in which he was so shortly again to play the leading part?

By 1915 he is alluded to in the letters of the Tsarina, recently published, as follows:

12th June 1915.

The rage of the officers against Sukhomlinoff is quite colossal – poor man, his very name they loathe, and yearn for him to be sent away; well, for his sake too, before any scandal arises, it would be better to do so. It is his adventurer wife who has completely ruined his reputation, because of her bribes he suffers and so on. One says it is his fault there is no ammunition, which is our great curse now.

General Sukhomlinoff is thus described by M. Paléologue, French Ambassador at the Court of the Tsar, on the outbreak of war:

> There is something about General Sukhomlinoff that makes one uneasy. Sixty-two years of age, the slave of a rather pretty wife, thirty-two years younger than himself, intelligent, clever, and cunning, obsequious towards the Tsar, and a friend of Rasputin, surrounded by a rabble who serve as intermediaries in his intrigues and duplicities; he is a man who has lost the habit of work and keeps all his strength for conjugal joys. With his sly look, his eyes always gleaming watchfully under the heavy folds of his eyelids, I know few men who inspire more distrust at first sight.

Eventually he was brought to trial on the charge of having betrayed his country, and he was sentenced to hard labour for life; he was held responsible for the shortage of munitions which so crippled Russia in the war, but Madame Sukhomlinoff was acquitted of complicity in the charges. Her adventures were not then ended, for rumour has it that the revolving wheel of political power again caught her, and she and her husband found themselves prisoners in the fortress of Peter and Paul, from whence she gallantly assisted him to escape. Having done so, she then annexed a young Georgian officer as his successor, and shared his tragic fate of being murdered by the Bolshevists.

At every station the Minister of War was received by all the officials of the district, bearing silver-topped wands of office, and accompanied by deputations, who made the customary offerings of bread and salt.

At one Cossack settlement he walked along the line of medalled men, and spoke a word to those specially decorated, while a hoarse rumble of a drilled cheer acknowledged him on departure. These Cossacks belong to various colonies whose ancestors were banished from Russia proper by Catherine the Great for their secession views regarding the Orthodox Church. Their chief objections were, to any retranslation of the Bible and to crossing with three fingers instead of two. They neither drink nor smoke, though the younger members seem to have lapsed from the stricter tenets of their ancestors. On the whole they appear to be a well-doing people, often stupid and inclined to be obstinate. At Orenburg there was a great display of a school of young Cossacks in blue-faced uniforms, who drew their swords in a dashing if somewhat perilous manner, and were inspected by the Minister, throwing into the shade a crowd of old men who had long forgotten any drill, and were stumbling with nervousness. The Minister's staff were gorgeous in grey and dark blue uniforms, and one had such a gigantic aigrette in his helmet that it threatened to blot out my kodak picture. The chief addressed words to most of the heads of deputations, and the band played as the train moved off, while from the humble obeisances of the peasants one would have thought that a god had come among them.

As we neared the Aral Sea at Kasalinsk signs were very evident that we were approaching the East in the crowd of Bokhara merchants in their picturesque robes, who had travelled north to offer a welcome. Oriental rugs were spread on the platform, red and white flags were fluttering around, and various officials were standing ready to make the usual offerings, while with them were rows of boys to be inspected. There was no attempt at uniform clothing among them, the only suggestion of such a thing being a belt! But in their ragged fur coats and caps they were ready to toss the latter and to give quite a joyful cheer. A group of venerable Abrahams with staves knelt and presented a petition, accompanied by a long oration of which it was said no one knew the purport. The nearer we approached Tashkent the more gorgeous were the officials, decked in velvet and gold lace, with heavily mounted silver and silver-gilt waistbands and buckles, small-swords, daggers all jewelled, medals, orders, and such-like splendours, while presentations of bread and salt were always forthcoming. At Tashkent a Cossack escort and band accompanied the General on his triumphal entry into the chief city of Turkestan.

XXIII

A Desert Emporium

*Accommodation – Hill Sanatorium – Rice
Cultivation – Flowery Roofs – Mosques and Colleges
– Climate – Marriage Market – Snuff-taking –
Life among the Kirghiz – A Leper Village*

A city in an empty land
Between the wastes of sky and sand.

Having seen the Minister of War and his cavalcade dash off in
fine style with a Cossack escort, I followed in a humbler fashion
by means of one, or rather two (very small) *isvostchiks* in waiting
at the station. This variety of carriage is also known under the
name of droshky in other parts of Central Asia, and somewhat
resembles a small high-set victoria with a hood. There being no
available accommodation in what was called the best hotel, I had
to be content with a room in a filthy inn, for which the propri-
etor had the effrontery to charge five shillings a day with no
attendance.

The first night that I made my bed I tried to remember how
this was done by Red Cross nurses (for this was in pre-war days),
but in spite of all efforts at recollection there seemed something
odd in the look of it; however, in the watches of the night came a

flash of inspiration – the result perhaps of discomfort, for I found that beneath my quilt I was lying on the springs of the bed, with no mattress.

Tashkent is the largest and most important city of the Russian possessions in Central Asia, and really consists of two cities: the modern town built since 1865, with a population of between 70,000 and 80,000 inhabitants, and the native one, some three miles distant, once united to the other by a horse tram service, since converted to an electric service. In order to supply the electricity required, a generating station had to be erected with powerful engines, as there was no system of electric lighting through the town. The trams were made up of first- and second-class carriages, costing a penny halfpenny and a penny a ride. The population of the native city was said to be about 100,000, but in all Eastern towns it is exceedingly difficult to get an accurate idea of the number of human beings they contain, as such reckoning is contrary to the precepts of Mahomet, who forbade any numbering of the people.

In order to gain some idea of the situation of Tashkent, let us on the map ascend the course of the River Syr Daria, the ancient Jaxartes, which flows into the Aral Sea, and twelve hundred miles from the mouth of the river we find the town of Tashkent. Though not actually situated on the river, it is amply supplied with water from a rapid-running tributary, called the Tchirtchik, which is led through the town by two canals, named Bos and Salar. Without the water of this stream the country – that is to say, its yellow soil, called loess, which is extraordinarily fertile when irrigated – would be arid and desert. This same loess provides the dust which is one of the trials of Turkestan from May to October, dense enough even to obscure the view of the mountains, eight miles away. The source of Tashkent's supply of water comes from a chain of mountains, visible from Tashkent when the atmosphere is not too dusty, which forms part of Mount Alexander.

In the upper reaches of the River Tchirtchik, near the village of Britoncmoulla, there is a bridge leading to the valley of the small tributary, called the Tchimgane. The valley of this name is about sixty miles from Tashkent and leads up to a glacier, which is never, even in the height of summer, entirely melted.

Not far from this glacier the Russian Government built a military hospital, to which were sent patients requiring special treatment, and particularly those suffering from malaria. This sanatorium has proved a great boon, for it is the only health station within reach, and if not always effecting a cure it can at least better the condition of the patients.

The inhabitants of Tashkent have obtained temporary concessions of land in the neighbourhood, and have built wooden huts on them which are so numerous as almost to suggest the idea of a second sanatorium. The journey thither, none too luxurious, is done in *arbas*, whose creaking wheels never seem to be oiled, or else it is performed in droshkys, and the poor invalids must be thankful to reach the end of a very long day by such a truly uncomfortable means of transport.

The chief contributing cause of the prevalent malaria is the cultivation of rice, which is done to a great extent in the environs of Tashkent, on the low-lying ground of both sides of the River Tchirtchik, from which the rice-fields are easily irrigated. These are divided into squares by ridges of mud piled up, and the top row of squares, which is higher, is first flooded and the water gradually let out into the successive rows till all is covered for the necessary length of time. It was on account of this cause of fever that the situation of the town was selected, seven miles from the

Tchirtchik, and forty miles from the little village of Tchinase on the Syr Daria.

The native city covers a considerable extent of ground, as most of the mud-houses are of one storey only; they are built around a court with a garden attached, which is protected by a mud wall. Windows on the street side are rarely seen, and any outlook is to the back. The roofs are flat, and also made of plastered mud, which is mixed with chopped straw, so that when spring reigns it is a pleasant and delightful surprise to see them covered with masses of poppies and other field flowers. The walls of the houses are constructed of large sun-dried bricks, raised on a foundation of stone from the bed of the River Tchirtchik, firmly fixed in layers, and finally covered over with wet mud to keep them in place.

As regards the mosques, they are built quite differently, and are very large buildings formed of kiln-burned bricks, resting on wide and deep foundations, which are then laid with flat-shaped bricks about nine inches square and one and a half inches thick. They are cemented with lime, and as a rule they are original in design and outstanding features of the native town. The *medresses*, or native colleges, which are attached to the mosques, are built with equal care and skill, and consist of numerous cells adjoining one another but detached, and only one student occupies each room. They are built around a courtyard from where there is no door into the street. The *medresse* is really the native university, for it is frequented only by young men of a certain social standing.

The natives who have reached a certain point in education – that is, those who conduct public devotions, who teach, or who have made a pilgrimage to Mecca – are styled mullahs, or learned men, but only the few who have made the pilgrimage to the tomb of the Prophet have the right to wear a green turban, in distinction to the rest of the other natives, who wear white. The long doubled folds of muslin which form the turban are wound round a close-fitting stitched skull-cap, which is called a *tibitait*. When working at home or in the fields the turban is removed and only the cap is in evidence.

Men's heads are shaved, and as this operation has to be frequently performed a common sight to be met with in Old Tashkent is the itinerant barber who plies his trade in the open air.

The weather is at its best in March and April, and then again in September and October, as the summers are from all accounts unbearably hot and the winters usually wet, although for the last two years they have been bitterly cold with frost and snow. In the wet season no one dreams of going out without goloshes, and I associate with shops or public offices rows and rows of such footgear, with the initials of the owner in white metal inside on the heel of each. What a business I had to get mine; E.R.C. came out as G.S.H. Such are the idiosyncrasies of Russian letters, and as I knew I never should be able to recognize those as mine I had to accept another nomenclature. On wet days one can never attempt to cross the street except at the crossings, or one will leave both goloshes behind, and even shoes included; in fact one may be considered lucky to arrive at the other side with both feet, so adhesive is the mud.

Tashkent is a place difficult to describe, but with a fascination all its own, and its many interests never pall. What does, I think, strike one most on arriving for the first time is the wonderful blaze of colour. Even in winter the sky is of a bright blue, and cloudless, and a Turkestan sky has a hue that is unlike any other. It is always of a vivid transparency, and at night turns to a beautiful sapphire-blue. The gay colourings of the clothes worn by the Sarts (the natives of the town) and the Kirghiz, men, women and children, incessantly passing to and fro, lends interest to the scene, and hardly less attractive are their camels, which pad along, stately and quiet, while the tinkle of the camel bell often hanging from their necks gives a suggestion of the free life of the desert, as has been graphically described by Sir R. Burton:

> All other life is living death,
> A world where none but phantoms dwell;
> A break, a wind, a sound, a voice,
> A tinkling of the camel bell

to which is added the jingling of numerous strings of beads. As has been so truly said, ' "if" the camel is the ship of the desert,' the market towns on the margin of the sandy wastes are its ports. Their bazaars hold everything that the nomad needs, and their suburbs are a shifting series of shepherd encampments or extensive caravanserais for merchants and pack animals.

The Sarts ('Sart' means 'merchant') are a peaceable and industrious people, who form the merchant class, and dearly love driving a bargain. The bazaars in the old city are situated in narrow, winding streets, most of them covered over to keep them cool in the fierce heat of summer. Each street specializes in one class of goods, a custom practically always found in Eastern cities. In one only carpets and rugs are sold, in another leather, in another brass and copper for the sale of the long-necked ewers with lids. Among the many uses to which these ewers are put is that of pouring water over the hands after a meal – a necessary ablution when one realizes the balls of mutton-fat food the fingers of the diners have rolled and scooped up. After the watering process the hands then smooth down the thick and glossy beards of the men, but whether this is done to dry them, or to apply grease in a mild form to the beards, it is not easy to say.

A large part of the bazaar is devoted to what I may call the agricultural section, where grains of all kinds are sold, and I especially associate groups of Kirghiz hovering around in this quarter in order to supply their wants, which not infrequently take the shape of brightly painted wooden cradles with an arched top like a handle over which a rug can be thrown for warmth.

Barley is used for horse-feeding, wheat for making the native scone-like bread, and there is laid out in various large and small sacks an immense variety of other grains, of which rice, sorghum, millet and maize are only a few of the vast number exposed for sale.

Somewhere near one is sure to find tobacco, rock-salt, cotton, flax, hemp, of which an uncleaned kind called *kendir* is used in making ropes and cordage. The fibre of the native cotton being shorter and coarser than the American variety, this renders it more elastic and therefore more suitable for padding the quilts and garments in universal use. The cultivation of American cotton has in a great measure ousted that of native corn, thus limiting it to an area that was not adapted for the more profitable cotton crop.

Another street has dried fruits and raisins, not far off is the spice bazaar, next cotton and silk goods, and so on; in this way shopping is really made much easier than it would be otherwise, for even if it were only a question of purchasing perhaps one article one is obliged to spend the best part of a day in searching for it. Not that one's labour is ended in finding it; in fact it is only beginning. One starts at the first shop by offering about a third or less of what the seller asks for the coveted article, and by this act attracts the attention of all the other stall-holders in the street, who instantly yell in chorus that they can offer a much better sample; for the shops being open-fronted and the streets only eight to ten feet wide, it is not difficult to see and hear all that passes in the vicinity. The amount of time consumed by the purchase depends on the resolution and knowledge of the buyer, but it never can be described as short.

The Sart is always civil, and many bowls of tea are apt to be drunk before a purchase is completed. On any succeeding visit one is greeted like an old friend by the venders, as by that time they have got to know who one is and all one's family history! Of course the shops do not serve as dwellings but merely as booths, with the wooden-fronted shutters closed at night by two fixed rings and a primitive-shaped padlock, while watchmen parade the streets to guard against thieves.

The Sart women are seldom seen, and are closely veiled when they do appear. They are not even allowed the pleasure of shopping, as that is done for them by their husbands. The life of the Kirghiz woman is much less restricted, as they are not veiled, and they are allowed to walk about the bazaars and converse freely with their men friends. One strange feature in their existence is the Kirghiz marriage market held once a week. It is very interesting, though a sad performance to watch. From our point of view it seems inhuman, but one has to realize the entirely different outlook on life of these people, starting at the outset by the girl, as such, not being wanted; so probably for the first time she is a creature of some importance and value.

The Kirghiz parents bring their girls, aged from nine to twelve, into the market, where they are sold to the highest bidder – that means, whichever man can give the greatest number of camels, sheep, goats, etc., to the child's father. As to the little bride, she does not seem to feel more concern than a puppy would on being transferred to a new master. She may feel strange at first, but that is all. The chances of any affection being shown to her may be more, and certainly will not be less, in the new home than in the old.

In Bokhara a similar custom prevails, but there the transaction is done in private: a girl costs four hundred roubles, while a widow may be had for a hundred and fifty. The Sart marriages at Tashkent are arranged also in private; even on the birth of a girl she may be promised to a man then grown up; on her reaching the age of nine, ten, or twelve, the marriage ceremony will take place, when she will have to face her fresh surroundings.

The principal streets of the native town are paved with cobbles from the bed of the river, from which tiny streams of water are led down at least one side of the roadway, and in summer this supply of water serves to water the streets very primitively by means of a wooden scoop. The other method of laying the dust is by a water-carrier who carries on his back the skin of an animal filled with water. It is suspended by a rope which passes across his chest, and this obliges him to bend very much in walking, while he helps himself along by a short thick stick, that also seems to support the skin of water when he wishes to rest himself. He shoots out the water from the neck of the skin, while he manipulates the spraying with his fingers.

The natives are clever with their hands, good house-builders, skilful carpenters, industrious cultivators of the soil, and remarkably expert in managing the water supply necessary for the cultivation of their ground. Their axes and hatchets (*techa*) are of a practical form, as well as their long-handled spade (*tikmain*), which is shaped like a hoe and is very effective for the hard soil which it has to tackle, avoiding the necessity of excessive stooping over the ground, so familiar to us.

In the bazaar and near it are numerous houses called *tchai khans*, or tea-houses, where the weary may rest, and where the male portion of the population often assemble to eat, smoke, drink tea, and gossip, while they listen to loud-voiced gramophones, or native musicians twanging their stringed instruments. During working hours the natives, whether at home or in the fields, constantly drink very hot weak green tea, without sugar, or, if any be used, a tiny bit is placed on the tongue and the tea sucked through it. They take about with them small kettles in wrought copper, called *kouneganes*, with which to boil the water, and as they are easily carried they can be used by outdoor workers.

The native smokes only at intervals, and those occasions are rare; but when he does indulge he inhales very slowly and deeply three or four whiffs of smoke, which reaches his mouth through a long pipe-stem after it has bubbled through the water of a receiver, which is usually made of a dried gourd, or *chilim*. Tobacco is also used in another form. After it has been reduced to a fine powder (still retaining its original colour), it is slightly moistened and then put into small bottles made for the purpose, either of dried gourds or glass. These glass bottles are often of Chinese manufacture, and one that I purchased was such a perfect imitation of agate that its nature was only revealed after a suicidal attempt from off a table. The tobacco bottles are kept in one of the many encircling folds of the waistband. From time to time a small quantity of the powder is put in a little heap in the hollow of the hand and deftly thrown into the mouth under the tongue, and after being held there for a few minutes it is spat out. This manner of using tobacco, as a kind of narcotic, must be of very ancient origin, because only quite recently a celebrated Danish traveller found that Eskimos in Canada, who had never seen a white man, used it thus.

The children, generally speaking, look healthy, though eye troubles from infantile neglect are not uncommon. Boys and girls play together until about the age of seven, when they are separated.

The women as well as the men wear high soft leather boots, with a soled overshoe, which is slipped off on entering the door of a house. Only men wear the thick-soled boots which require no overshoes or goloshes. Men and women alike wear an undergarment of linen and cotton, which is of very coarse homespun material. The outer clothing of both sexes consists of a dressing-gown-like robe, crossed in front and kept in place by a waistband made of a long piece of coloured silk or wool material wound several times round the figure – a sensible form of dress in such a climate as Turkestan.

For winter wear these same shaped robes are padded with cotton, and their very long sleeves extend over the hands so that they can be tucked into the ends like a muff. One or more robes are worn according to the requirements of the temperature.

In addition to this the women, when they go out into the streets, wear another robe-like garment, which, resting on the crown of the head, serves to support the black horse-hair veil, a necessary article they are obliged to wear in order not to be seen of men. This veil is very wide and reaches to the waist, and the mesh is coarse enough for the wearer to see through it, though she herself may be invisible; while as the arms are not thrust through the sleeves of the robe it is tied together in front by a knotted cord in order to keep it in place. Coloured spectacles and even parasols frequently form part of the natives' dress, so as to afford protection from the dust and glare, which often causes eye troubles.

The settled population of Tashkent consists of Sarts and a few Tatars; but there are also a certain number of Kirghiz, who migrate to the town or near it, and there pitch their tents for the winter – 'a dome of laths and o'er it felts were spread.' As spring approaches they disappear to the steppes with troops of mares, which provide that nourishing and sustaining food called *koumiss*, and flocks of camels, whose legs are shackled to prevent them from straying, and which can thus be easily caught when required.

The chief occupation of the Kirghiz is to pasture vast flocks of sheep and to seek out those places where grass may be found to the animals' liking. As soon as night draws on the animals gather in from every side to their respective camps – 'the ox knoweth his owner and the ass his master's crib.' Their owners spend the night stretched on the ground on rugs or quilted coverlets, their feet turned towards a fire which is lighted in the centre of the tent and above which is an opening to allow of the smoke escaping. Powerful and savage watchdogs guard the flocks –

> Towards Merve,
> The Shiak dogs who pasture sheep,
> And up from thence to Urgenje

– accompanied by shepherds especially told off for this work, and all are grouped quite close to 'the black Toorkmun tents.'

The sheep of Turkestan, as in the rest of Central Asia, is the fat-tailed species (the tail is really only a fatty excrescence like the hump of a camel), of which the natural use seems to be to provide a store of nourishment for the animal when food is lacking on the steppes. Mutton forms the basis of food among all the natives, Sarts and Kirghiz alike. They eat it cut in little pieces about the size of one's thumb, six or eight pieces threaded upon a skewer: these are laid side by side over a clear fire made of heath, and with one hand furnished with a straw-made fan the *chef* ceaselessly blows away any smoke, while with the other hand he turns and re-turns the skewers until the meat is broiled, when he replaces them by others. These tit-bits are called *shashlik*.

The most common food of the population is *pilau*, which is rice cooked in a certain manner with mutton fat, to which is added small bits of the meat, shreds of carrots, quince, and raisins, and is also an acceptable dish to Europeans.

Sweets and jams are liked, and a great deal of fruit is dried in the sun, both for home consumption and for exportation; but in the latter category cotton is by far the most important product; then follow others, such as raw and manufactured silk, dried fruits, wool, skins, felt rugs, and rock-salt.

In the native city are numerous bath-houses, but, unlike our idea of a bath, the floor is cement and heated from beneath, and water is poured upon it so as to raise a steam. The bather washes first with hot water in a basin and then with cold, but does not plunge into the water.

The march of civilization has brought sewing machines, and they are extensively used in the making of men's clothing. The shops are lighted by petrol lamps, but one may still see primitive or classical forms of small pottery lamps and dishes or tumblers with floating wicks.

For travelling, *arias*, or high-wheeled native carts, are in general use for the transport of women, children and goods, when the latter are not conveyed on camels.

The Russians have opened dispensaries which are largely taken advantage of, as connected with them are both men and women doctors who hold consultations at certain hours, and vaccinate the children brought to them, while nurses are in attendance to do the necessary dressings, and patients can even be X-rayed. A chemist's shop forms part of the dispensary equipment, in order to provide the natives with the remedies prescribed for them. Another beneficent work was the gathering together of all lepers in a village especially built for them. They were employed on agricultural labour on lands allotted to them, and the few who were allowed into the town had to walk in the middle of the road, wearing bells so that people might know who they were. Formerly they were scattered among the healthy population and used to subsist by going around with a metal bowl into which the charitable would drop a coin. I understand that under the present regime of so-called socialist freedom the lepers are again seen everywhere and are no longer confined to their village. Up to the age of ten the children of lepers look quite healthy, and one would never imagine they bore within them the seeds of so dreadful and fatal a malady.

XXIV

Tashkent, Past & Present

A Novel Capitulation – The Emperor's Half – A New Town – Library – Hospital Accommodation – A Strange Fish – Churches – Oil Fuel – Country Produce

The origin of the city of Tashkent is veiled in mystery. From the writings of Hionen-Thsang in the tenth century we know that a city did exist on the site of what is now Old Tashkent, but its name underwent various modifications, and finally its present form was evolved from the Turkish nomadic tribes, who found that the name *Skash*, as it was then termed, meant nothing to them, so they changed it into *Task*, a stone, and *kent*, from the Persian word signifying a city. Hence we may gather that it was even in those days a place of some consequence and therefore raised above the mean level of a mud encampment.

The possession of Tashkent fluctuated between the Emirs of Bokhara, Samarkand, and nomadic tribes, and its fortunes were various.

In the march of conquest by Ginghiz Khan, Tashkent was in the line of fire, so to speak; it was therefore appropriated by him and ruled by his successors until the reign of Tamerlane, when he and his descendants had a period of sovereignty.

The Kirghiz then entered on possession, and retained the city for a hundred years, until 1759, when it passed under the sway of the Emir of Bokhara, and was governed alternately from Bokhara and Khokand until the conquest by Russia in 1865, under the forces of General Tchernaief, who afterwards acted as Governor.

This honour gained by General Tchernaief was not achieved without formidable opposition on the part of the Emir of Khokand, supported by the Emir of Bokhara. Neither of these two native rulers finding great favour with the inhabitants, a deputation of the more important and peaceful members presented themselves to General Tchernaief and surrendered the city unconditionally, while at the same time they issued a proclamation which they asked the General to sign. As it must be almost unique in the annals of capitulations, I venture to quote parts of it:

'By order of the great White Tsar, and by command of his lieutenant, the Governor Iskander Tchernaief [this is a compliment referring to Alexander the Great, the General's name being Michael], we hereby declare to the inhabitants of the city of Tashkent that they must in everything act according to the commands of Almighty God, and the teaching of the orthodox religion of Mohammed, on whom and on whose descendants be the blessing of God, and to the laws established by him, not departing from them one iota. Let all, so far as they can, act for the advantage and profit of the country. Let them say everywhere their prayers five times a day, not passing by the appointed time an hour or even a minute. Let the mullahs constantly go to their schools and teach the laws of the Mohammedan faith, and not waste the time of their pupils by an hour or by a minute. Let children not for one hour miss their lessons, and let the teachers try to collect the children in school, and not give them hours of idleness, and in case of need use strong measures, even beating, to make them learn, and if the parents show careless-ness in this let them in accordance with the Mohammedan *Shariat* be brought to the Reis, the head of the city, or Kazi Kilian, and be well punished. Let the inhabitants of the country occupy themselves with their work. Let the people of the bazaar carry on their trade and not pass their time idly. Let every man carry on his own work. Let nothing be thrown into the streets, and let them be kept clean. All the inhabitants of Tashkent, rich and poor, must exactly fulfil all that has been said above. Houses, gardens, fields, lands, and watermills, of which you have possession, will remain your property. The soldiers will take nothing from you. You will not be made Russian Cossacks. There will be no quartering of soldiers on you. No soldier will come into your courtyards, or if he come let us know at once, and he will be punished. Great kindness is shown to you and therefore you should pray for the health of the White Tsar. If anyone kill anybody, or rob a merchant, he will be judged by Russian laws. If anyone kill himself, his property goes to his heir according to the *Shariat*; we will take none of his property. The tenth part which is taken from the products of Government land, I, the Governor Iskander Tchernaief, remit to you for the present year, but afterwards it will be in accordance with the will of our great white Tsar to show you according to his own disposition still greater kindness' – 2nd July 1865, with the Mahometan date attached.

From this document a great mending of manners seems to have been designed to be carried on, especially the emphasis laid on wasting time, such a characteristic failing of the East, where noth-ing – notably not street cleaning! – seems to be done to-day that could possibly be put off till the morrow. But if he who aims high shoots the higher for it, though he shoot not as high as he aim, let us hope that the streets of Tashkent were a little less dirty than they would have been without the proclamation!

For General Tchernaief himself the people had nothing but admiration, and from the tactful way in which he assumed command and sympathetically fell in with native customs, his courage earned for him his name transposed into Shir-naib, or 'the lion viceroy.'

To him fell the honour of formally annexing the town of Tashkent in 18 6?, and that having been achieved, he speedily set to work to lay out a modern city on really imposing lines, with avenues of trees, public parks and gardens, all worthy of an important capital. For a long time the growth of this new town was very slow. This was partly caused by its remoteness from Russia, and the lack of transport thither; then the vast stretches of quite uncultivated and apparently unproductive land did not attract colonists, who also had to face the lack of water, while the many days of desert travelling from Russia to the north of the Aral Sea formed an almost insuperable barrier to any progress.

It was only after the taking of Samarkand, and later the conquest of Khiva and Transcaspia, with a Turcoman population, that Turkestan was fully consolidated, and that the question arose of determining where its capital should be. At first it was thought to restore to Samarkand the position of capital of the country which it occupied in the time of Tamerlane (1336-1405); but that idea had to be given up because the small river, the Zerafshan, from which was drawn the water supply for the country district had first to supply Bokhara, and therefore great extensions to the city were rendered impossible.

A curious fact to be noted is that the Zerafshan, the little River Mourghab, as well as the River Tchou, with its source near the great lake of Issik-Kul, are streams that do not discharge themselves into any other body of water, for they and their tributaries are lost in cultivated lands that can absorb all the water that is conveyed to them. The real development of Tashkent only began under General Kauffmann, a personal friend of the Tsar Alexander II., who governed with full powers, and for that reason the natives gave him the nickname of Tarime Fadicha (the Emperor's half). Kauffmann built a governor's palace, where he lived in great state, and never left it except accompanied by an escort of a hundred Cossacks who bore a royal standard unfurled in front of him.

In 1876 plans were adopted for the further laying out of the new town. With a noble foresight the streets were made wide (the principal ones are not less than seventy yards), with avenues of trees – acacia, poplar and elm – and rills of water flowing between the rows of trees, while the roads are macadamized. The principal park was planted with black elm and other trees, while avenues radiated from the centre square in the town, where was erected the monument to General Kauffmann, on which was inscribed his words: 'I pray you bury me here, that everyone may know that this is true Russian earth, in which no Russian need be ashamed to lie.'

In the vast and beautiful public park came the usual Russian incongruity of ideas – at the entrance gate on the principal avenue was an isolated glass case in which were two pairs of the newest cut of corsets mounted on stands! Nowhere else could that have been seen except in Russia. Some especially heavy bribe must have secured this post of vantage.

The military, forming an important item in the government of Turkestan, were provided with large barracks for the soldiers, and there was also a very fine club for the officers, attached to which was a theatre, a library, reading and other rooms, all surrounded by an extensive garden.

The town library, founded by General Kauffmann, was considered to have the finest collection of books on Turkestan in the world, besides all ethnographical information in the form of pictures and photographs. It contained reading-rooms where the chief newspapers in Russian, French, English, German and Polish were accessible, as well as Russian and other European illustrated papers. For scientists there was a well-appointed institution for the study of cartography and topography, with a repairing plant at hand for all scientific instruments that might be required for that special branch of study. As the clear atmosphere was peculiarly favourable for the study of astronomy, there was a splendid observatory with a revolving roof situated in a spot just outside the town, equipped with one of the three largest telescopes in Russia, besides other astronomical telescopes and a seismograph, and there was a special library treating of those subjects, while the scientific staff found accommodation in a cluster of separate houses near by, built expressly for their occupation.

At the risk of this being mistaken for a guide-book I must proceed with a further list of public buildings in order to show what had been accomplished under the old regime. There was a large civil hospital, and one under the auspices of the Red Cross, with their own water supply brought from an artesian well, the sinking of which was a private enterprise. A military hospital saw to the medical requirements of the soldiers, and there was one for electric treatment by which the public might also benefit, while standing in its own beautiful grounds, about half-a-mile out of the town, was an enormous lunatic asylum.

In a museum, founded by General Kauffmann – I have a vivid recollection of its dust and total lack of arrangement – my attention was caught by some curious carved stone hands from an old mosque in Andijan. There was also a heap of water-washed stones, with a cross roughly scratched on them, and a name – sometimes two names, one on each side of the cross, one the baptismal and the other the heathen: these were all relics of the Nestorian Church of the seventh century, and are rare in this part of Turkestan.

In the natural history section I was shown a bottle containing a fish with a long rat-looking tail, known as the *scaphiryncus*, living in the Amu Daria and the Amazon only, as my kind guide, Colonel Viartzin, informed me, adding he knew 'it was a river in America, but it might have been the Mississippi'; as to this I leave scientists to decide.

As to churches, most religions are well represented. Among the Russian there is a very imposing cathedral with its five domes, all solidly built to withstand earthquake shocks, which are not uncommon in these parts, while Protestants and Catholics as well as Jews all have their own respective buildings. Of schools there are many; as far back as 1878 academies were erected for both boys and girls with boarding accommodation. Then followed a seminary for the preparation of Russian teachers for schools for natives, all showing a high standard in the education of youth.

Signs of industry and commerce are not lacking. Of factories there are four or five for the cleaning of cotton and separating it from the seed before the raw material is compressed into bales for export to Europe, and a very good tasteless oil is expressed from the cotton seed by an American process, which is used for cooking purposes. The refuse of the seed as well as that of flax, and the waste produce of breweries and sugar-canes, are all used in the feeding of cattle. A great deal of lucerne is employed for this, especially when dried like hay, and the animals are also given barley, bran, wheat, straw chopped fine, small quantities of oats, and even rice straw.

The fuel that is burned to provide the motor power of the tramway station and factories is a black liquid called *mayoute*. It is obtained by boring in various desert districts of Ferghana and elsewhere, but it is also extracted as a by-product from other minerals, such as petrol. Coal is found in very limited quantities in the country, chiefly in the eastern districts, and the houses are warmed by central heating from stoves which from their construction throw out a great deal of heat, and this gradually penetrates to the rooms with their double windows; these are necessary in a winter that lasts two to three months, with a temperature that has been known to fall as low as 17° Reaumur. Wood is generally consumed in these stoves, as well as in the kitchen one; apricot, mulberry, willow and plane supply the logs, though sometimes coal of an inferior kind can be obtained to help out the cooking arrangements.

The chief streets have an imposing aspect, from the number of large and fine houses with which they are lined, many of them standing apart in their own walled-in gardens. The roofing of the houses generally consists of felt or painted iron. The interior both of the Russian and Sart houses is lighted by excellent petrol lamps of from five to twenty-six candle-power, and similar lamps also illuminated the streets, though after the electric station was installed for the tramway service electric light was gradually introduced, and a telephone service was in full working order.

The drainage system seemed to me very sketchy, in fact I almost doubted the existence of any, and water seemed to be largely drawn from wells or canals: again the usual Russian extremes and stopping short of great beginnings, but perhaps in their system they reverse the order of what we are accustomed to consider essentials.

There was a Treasury where State papers were kept, a Government Bank, and two private ones. As regards shopping, there was a Russian bazaar in the new town, where things of the most varied description could be purchased – and if tidiness were the keynote of the Sart bazaar in the old city, certainly here it was the very opposite; in contrast to the quiet of the one across the canal, the Russian bazaar was like Bedlam. It was held in a large open space near the centre of the town, and the kiosks were mostly owned by small shopkeepers.

The more important streets had some very good shops, where provisions could be had very cheap. A good-sized chicken cost about sixpence, and a hundred eggs could be bought for about one and fourpence, while milk and butter were correspondingly reasonable; at the same time what seemed simple wants were unobtainable. Having profited by a previous experience, I decided to take with me a supply of butter for future use, as after Tashkent I knew I should have no further opportunity of getting any. I entered a very superior shop that sold only butter, bacon and cheese, and purchased some pounds of excellent Siberian butter, and mentioned that I should like it put into jars. This was unheard of, no butter was ever sold except in paper, and I was assured no shop in Tashkent could produce anything else. I spent a whole morning between china-shops and fancy bazaars in search of jars without any success. At last a house-painter was suggested as possibly being able to supply something like what I required. I laughed at the idea, but, knowing that it is always the unexpected that happens in Russia, I made for his shop. All he could furnish were some tins that had contained linseed oil, but as those were the first receptacles of any kind that I had struck, except celluloid soap-boxes, I decided to take them. I made Fritz scald them with soda and boiling water, and after lining them well with paper the butter merchant filled them, and we had then to take them to an artisan who could solder the tins. This gives some idea of what shopping meant, as a whole day was occupied over this one transaction, but I can still recall the glow of satisfaction with which it was concluded. There were some very ambitious shops for Paris clothes (so they were called) and hats, but everything of that kind was very expensive; which was hardly to be wondered at when one considered the distance that Tashkent was from any large centre, which made the cost of freight so exceedingly heavy.

European life was quite gay. There was a Governor-General and a Governor, with a large military society, and the Russians, who are among the most hospitable people in the world, entertained lavishly. There was a very fine winter theatre, and a summer one in the park, which had quite good dramatic companies from Petrograd and Moscow for the season. There was also a hippodrome, a form of entertainment greatly favoured by both Russians and natives. Indeed in the various native cities it was no uncommon sight to find on a vacant space that a band of strolling acrobats, or a man with a tame bear or performing dogs, had taken up their position, with admiring crowds in a circle round them. Indeed on one occasion I found that a turbaned Sart, with a comic cast of countenance, seated on a minute donkey had, thanks to the gullibility of his onlookers, gathered quite a number round him to watch the acrobatic performances of a tame jackdaw on a stick!

XXV

A Russian Easter

A Monster Cake – Easter Eve – A Stately Procession –
Blessing of Bread – Matrimonial Market – Cheap Driving

I retain quite a joyful remembrance of an Easter spent at Tashkent, thanks in large measure to the kindness of Monsieur and Madame Müller. He had occupied important posts in the educational department of the province, and had then retired and settled permanently in Tashkent. His family consisted of four lusty daughters, Valentine, Germaine, Jeanne, and Alice, all Russian in appearance in spite of their mother being French and their father Swiss, and typical of what environment can effect. All the girls collected picture post cards, and were proud to accept of 'Auld Reekie' and the Adonises of Highland regiments, not to speak of a fine thistle bristling at every prickle with 'Wha daur meddle wi' me?' I shared their hospitality more than once, and for supper one evening we had as a centre-piece an enormous Easter cake, which I could honestly praise as it was so deliciously light, and I remarked that such success could not be achieved without the expenditure of many eggs. 'Yes,' said Madame calmly, 'I put eighty-five into the batch.' And those were eggs of normal size! A succession of samovars kept all the party occupied drinking tumblers of straw-coloured tea and talking; this was continued until ten P.M. Having seen no newspaper for a fortnight, I asked if there were any special news chronicled. According to the Russian newspaper the most recent information reported from Europe was that '*Guillaume et le Lord avait une conférence au sujet de la flottille anglaise!*'

On Easter Eve I went to the Russian church to attend the midnight service. Crowds of people were flocking outside the church, while inside it was filled to suffocation. The wealthier female members were all attired in their newest French fashions, for Tashkent is a very 'dressy' place, while some had almost reached the pitch of evening gowns without hats.

In the midst of all the crowd outside fireworks and squibs were let off at intervals, adding to the noise and general air of excitement that prevailed. The singing, as in all Russian churches, was good, and the voices entirely unaccompanied. At intervals during the service the priests, who wore gorgeous vestments, had to remove their ecclesiastical hats, and some were evidently very much afraid that their flowing locks might be disarranged in the process. Hands were surreptitiously raised to smooth any possible ruffling of their carefully arranged 'braids,' and I even saw a pocket comb being applied to a Titian-red head.

After that part of the service was over in the church we all went outside to take part in the procession which parades three times round the building, each one carrying a lighted wax taper. A stranger kindly provided me with one, and as I look back on that function it seems to me almost a miracle that someone was not set alight, especially the wearers of large gauze hats. I felt all the time ready to cry out: '*Mais qui est-ce qui me brûle?*'

The next item, one may say on the programme, was the blessing of bread, brought by those who desired a comprehensive benediction on their basket and on their store. The finest and most elaborate cakes, a lighted taper fixed in each one, were set out in a circle, the owners kneeling behind, also with a lighted taper, ready to be blessed by the priest as he passed along in full canonicals. All this, with the blaze of lights, made a most striking effect in the dusk.

After the procession was over the crowd returned to the church, but I left before the promiscuous kissing began, though less of this is now done. Each salute was accompanied by the words, 'Christ is risen,' with the reply, 'He is risen indeed.'

Every officer had to kiss his men three times, while the officiating priest came in for a large share, and was the first to be so greeted.

The following day I dined with the Müllers, the hour being four P.M., but the meal was interrupted the whole time by the arrival of callers, for it is the custom for all men to call upon their friends on Easter Day, while the women do so on the following afternoon, and each individual on entering was introduced to everyone present in the room, and shook hands all round.

Not less ceremonious were their clothes: one was in full evening dress even to a white tie, another was in a frock-coat and checked morning trousers, another wore Russian uniform, while he was speedily followed by a huge Pole, to whom M. Müller described my travels, which had included a trip to India. I do not know what may have been the golden vision of the matrimonial market across the Himalayas as pictured in Tashkent, but all he remarked as he turned on his heel was: 'What i she has been to India and not even found a husband there!'

The *pièce de résistance* of the dinner was – a leg of veal. Madame carved it herself, cutting the slices down the leg. Mercifully I did not allude to it as a leg of mutton, which I was on the point of doing but stopped in time. Then followed an enormous open apple-tart about the size of a tea-tray, accompanied by cream cheese which was sweetened and flavoured with vanilla. This sounds an odd mixture, but the result was excellent. The meal was washed down by the red wine of the country as well as muscatel, with tea and coffee as a finish.

The callers just sat on, watching us eat, smoked a cigarette, and then continued their round of calls. We had music after feasting: Caucasian airs, which much resemble Scotch reels, and the picture of the sword dance seemed quite familiar.

Drivers have a busy time at Easter, as no one makes calls on foot; but their fares are cheap, and although the droshkys are very small, barely seating two with comfort, they all have two horses. The winter tariff is about sixpence a course, and the summer one is reduced by one penny and no tips.

XXVI

The Town of Turkestan

*Tamerlane's Last Building – A Saint's Tomb
– Persian Art – Bronze Treasures*

Having a desire to see the last great mosque erected by Tamerlane,
I arranged by means of an early morning start from Tashkent to
stop for a day at the town of Turkestan on my return journey to
Russia.

Soon after leaving the cultivated area around Tashkent one
enters on more or less of a desert journey, the monotony of which
is broken only by Kirghiz huts and brackish lakes, until the neighbourhood of the town of Turkestan is reached, where the green of
its trees and orchards proclaims that the work of irrigation is in
progress. As a Sart proverb says: 'Drop upon drop makes a sea, but
where there are no drops there is a desert.' Although formerly the
capital of the province of Turkestan, until 1864, when that honour
was bestowed on Tashkent, the town was in a derelict condition,
and far from even attempting to assume the official honour thrust
upon it, or of presenting the appearance that might have been
expected from the city named after such an important province.
With the advent of the Russians in 1864 some revival of interest
and occupation took place, and a well laid-out Russian town was
built some three miles from the railway station. I suppose the

three miles were left for possible expansion of the town, but when I saw it its dusty track was occupied only by camels, sheep, and goats, which were engaged in trying to pick up a scanty livelihood on its arid surface.

The native town, once of considerable size, is now merely a collection of mud-huts. There is a bazaar, with native citizens at work, hammering brass and copper, and chiselling, or rather engraving, by means of elementary tools the decoration of a simple kind that supplies the artistic wants of the people.

The chief object of interest is the mosque built over the tomb of Hazret Hodja Akhmed Yasair. He was one of the most celebrated Moslem saints of Central Asia, who founded the sect Jahria, and is the special patron of the Kirghiz. He died some time about 1120. Tamerlane when on one of his numerous wedding journeys halted at the town of Turkestan to greet his new bride, Tukel Cannen, and while waiting for her arrival his active brain conceived the idea of building this mosque, perhaps one of the largest erected during his reign, and a fitting conclusion to his architectural record. The front consists of burnt brick firmly put together, and probably the original intention was to face it with coloured tiles; but this idea was never carried out. Tamerlane died, and his death-knell sounded the cessation of all such ambitious building projects. In the front wall may be seen the holes for the scaffolding, now the homes of birds, and even some of the beams still remain: many centuries have passed since the day that the workmen laid down their tools, possibly unaware that never again would they be required.

On the back part of the building and the sides the tiles remain in a very damaged condition, and what were vacant spaces have been but roughly filled in. The central portal, or *piktash*, is about eighty feet in height, and at each corner of the façade are towers with battlemented tops, a reminder of the time when the mosque from its commanding height served as a fortress. The building is crowned by a huge dome, once covered with blue fluted tiles, of which only fragments appear through the cement repairs laid on by the Russians. Around the dome is a band inscribed in ornamental Cufic lettering, on which can still be read by skilled scholars that it was 'the work of Hodja Hussein, a native of the city of Shiraz.' Texts from the Koran in similar ornamental characters run round the frieze.

Beneath the fluted dome is the great hall, about a hundred feet in height, and its decorative plaster-work which covers the vast roof and wall space reminds one of early Moorish work in Spain. Around are various rooms containing tombs of numerous Kirghiz khans, and beneath the smaller dome at the back of this hall is the resting-place of him who was the unconscious originator of Tamerlane's last triumph, Akhmed Yasair; his family are included in the honour done to their head, and lie around him. There are other tombs of less interest, but only one claims attention – namely, that of a great-granddaughter of Tamerlane, daughter of the famous Ulea Beg. She was married to the then reigning khan of the country, and died in 1485. One of her sons is buried next to her.

In the centre of the great hall there stands a magnificent bronze 'laver,' as the Interpreter would call it – one of his many Biblical expressions – capable of holding about fifty gallons of water, for the use of pilgrims and those residing in the mosque. It stands on a pedestal – the combined height is 5 feet 4 inches – and was cast in five portions; poles with standards and bunches of horsehair are fastened to it in supporting positions, while the outside of the basin is covered by inscriptions moulded and chiselled, which are now only partially legible, but the following can still be deciphered: 'The highest and Almighty God said: "Do ye place those bearing water to pilgrims and visiting the sacred temple. May peace be on him. Whoso sets a vessel of water for the sake of God, the Highest, him will God the Highest reward doubly in Paradise." By command of the great Amir, the ruler of nations chosen by the care of the most merciful God, the Amir Timur Gurgan. May God prolong his reign!'

Another part of the inscription honours the artist, or at least makes his name immortal: 'The work of the servant, striving Godward, the Abdul-aziz, son of the master Sheref-uddin, native of Tabriz.' This shows that up to the end of his life Tamerlane was indebted to Persian artists and art in the execution of his many memorials.

In the same hall are four very fine bronze candelabra, also the work of a Persian artist from Ispahan in the year 1397. Schuyler says: 'This mosque is considered the holiest in all Central Asia, and had very great religious importance, as previous to the capture of the city even khans and amirs assembled there from all quarters. In the taking of the city by the Russians it was not spared artillery fire, as shown by the marks on the wall, and had a white flag not been flown from a minaret it is probable that little or none of it would have been left. The doors, carved and inlaid with mother-of-pearl, were removed to Petrograd and copies of them substituted.

'The mosque is entirely supported by property which has been given to it by various worshippers, including the revenues from several caravanserais and shops in the city, and very large amounts from land. Pilgrims are in the habit of offering sheep every Friday, the meat of which is distributed to the poor of the city.'

With reference to the prefix of the saint's name it is interesting to know that 'the word *Hazret*, an Arabic word, meaning literally 'presence,' is used in the sense of 'majesty' for rulers, and with the meaning 'sanctity' is frequently applied to saints, especially to those most reverenced, and in this case the celebrity of the saint has even given a name to the town, which is often called 'Hazreti-Turkestan,' or even simply 'Hazret.'

XXVII

Conclusion

*Bolshevist Teaching – Wholesale Slaughter – A
Dead Town – Confiscation – School Management
– Terrorized Natives – Departed Splendour*

In concluding my tale of two visits to Turkestan, written down, I
am afraid, with a very unprofessional pen, I cannot close this book
without some reference to the terrible events which have taken
place there during the last five years.

So overwhelming a record of slaughter and bloodshed has
filtered through, accompanied by such a hecatomb of suffering,
that for any parallel we must revert to the days of Ginghiz Khan,
or even earlier. Need we wonder at such results when we realize
what Bolshevik teaching means. At Ashkabad, now. known as
Poltaratsk, the motto inscribed over the door of the Bolshevik
First Army headquarters ran: 'Our mission is to set the East in
flames.'

Of what is actually remaining of the towns our information is
but scanty. We know that in 1918 the Mahometans of Tashkent,
Khokand, and Bokhara revolted against the Soviet Government.
In all three cities the rising was suppressed with great slaughter.
Khokand, the commercial city of wealth and prosperity, according
to reports, has been laid flat by high-explosive shell-fire and

30,000 beings massacred. In Bokhara much of the beauty of its buildings has been irreparably destroyed, and the letter which I now quote from Tashkent speaks for itself.

Dr Wilhelm Hahn was an Austrian who lived for five years in Tashkent as a prisoner of war. He was then compelled to serve in the Red Army. He arrived in 1916 and left in 1921:

'When I arrived in Tashkent it was a garden city of striking beauty, with modern shops, carriages, motor-cars, with the life of a small European capital. What has the October revolution made of Tashkent? To-day it is a dead and filthy town, where nothing remains to remind us of her pristine beauty. The shops are all empty and closed, and they have generally been transformed into Soviet offices. The whole trade of the East has come to an end. One never sees those interminable caravans of camels, whose countless processions once filled the streets of Tashkent with their joyful bells. Hotels, restaurants, and cafés are equally closed. The tram-cars have ceased to run. There is no more lighting of the streets. Everywhere we have the same picture of destruction and devastation. Cotton-growing in Turkestan for the last three years has almost ceased, but wheat is being sown to save the country from starvation. In all other districts in Bokhara and Khiva the war with the rebellious native tribes continues without interruption. And thus this once so fertile country is reduced to utter ruin.'

In that town a friend of mine was unfortunately caught in the wave of revolution and experienced the results of a Bolshevist government, but luckily was enabled to escape with her life, after unforgettable experiences. As in the early days of the history of that country there was wholesale pillage and robbery, for after all robbery is robbery whether the act be stealing from a poor man or one better off. Houses were forcibly taken possession of, whether they were the result of hardly earned savings and lifelong industry or not, and their contents appropriated, even to wearing apparel. An owner of a house got one room to live in and one change of clothing. For example, in a twelve-roomed house twelve families were huddled together, quite irrespective of any decent conditions of life. The one kitchen of the house was supposed to meet the wants of all those twelve families. A pot had to be watched on the stove or it was speedily removed, and in many cases was never seen again, as all classes, the worthy and the worthless, were compelled to congregate together. As an instance of this communal life a man and his wife and three children were the occupants of one room, and in order to give a little better accommodation for the children he arranged the beds like bunks, one above the other. He was promptly told by the authorities that he now had spare accommodation, so another family was thrust in on the top of them.

The schools are under what is called a Soviet Government of the children themselves, who make their own rules, engage and dismiss their teachers, close the schools when they like or keep them open to all hours, while the classrooms are filled with the heavy and poisonous fumes of *mahorka*, which is smoked during lesson hours by the pupils. One can picture the results of all this upon undisciplined and uncontrolled atoms of humanity. Immorality is rampant, and there is no guiding force to impel a better order for the direction of young lives.

The fine avenues of trees are now only a memory, for in the winter of 1919–1920, when the revolution was at its height in Turkestan, no fuel could be brought into Tashkent owing to the railway service being completely disorganized. The Soviet authorities had then to fall back upon the timber growing in the city, and these trees were therefore allotted to householders, who had to cut down his or her own tree; to some were allotted only branches, and these less fortunate ones had to chop and chip as best they could, for the bulk of tools, such as axes, had been commandeered by the Soviet Government, being reckoned as capital. This modicum of firewood was all they got for cooking purposes or heating their houses; perhaps one should rather say rooms, for by that time if one possessed a room that was considered a very great bit of luck.

The monument of the famous Russian general Kauffmann is also a thing of the past. It was taken down by the Soviet Government, and busts of Lenin and Trotsky erected instead; but these must have been made of very flimsy material, for they were short-lived, and the heavy rains washed them away bit by bit till little more than the pedestals were left. Is this typical of Soviet construction in general?

The palace of the Grand Duke Nikola has now been turned into a museum, and his widow (for he died shortly after the commencement of the revolution) has been made caretaker and guide to the public who frequent it, and as a concession she has been given a tiny space under the staircase where she is allowed to live. All the houses of the wealthy Russians, and afterwards of rich and poor alike, were taken from them; in other words, confiscated by the Bolsheviks, who either looted or destroyed things to such an extent (furniture, etc.) that they were afterwards of very little use to anyone.

A friend of mine who knew Tashkent well now writes to me: 'Tashkent to-day is not the Tashkent it was. The old feeling of peace, that "Bible scene" atmosphere, has gone. The natives keep to their own part of the city, as they are afraid to bring goods to the Russian town, knowing well the consequences; and everything in the Russian town has been spoilt as much as possible by Bolshevism. Its traces are everywhere; even the people seem to have undergone a sad change; and so they have, of course: no one can live under Soviet rule and remain the same. The Communist schools – what hope for the young generation? But this subject alone might make a book, and I would like to think only of Tashkent as it was before it was inoculated with the poison of Bolshevism!'

As has so ably been said by one of Russia's poets on the occasion when war threatened the country from without, now much worse when the enemy is from within:

> But war has spread its terrors o'er thee,
> And thou wert once in ashes laid;
> Thy throne seem'd tottering then before thee,
> Thy sceptre feeble as thy blade.
> Sarmatian fraud and force, o'er raging
> The humbled world, have reached thy gate;
> Thy faith with flattering smiles engaging,
> Now threatening daggers on thee wait –
> And they were drawn – thy temples sank –
> Thy virgins led with fetter clank –
> Thy sons' blood streaming to the skies –
> 'Spirit of Vengeance! now arise.
> Save me, thou guardian angel! Save!'
> So cried'st thou in thy agony.
> Thy streets are silent as the grave –
> The unsheath'd sword – it hangs o'er thee.
> And where is Russia's saviour – where? –
> Stand up – arouse thee – in thy might!'
>
> IVAN DMITRIEV

From the Foreign Office we learn that the National Soviet Republic of Bokhara has recently become a Socialist republic with the title of 'Socialist Soviet Republic of Bokhara,' and that a redistribution of Soviet territory in Central Asia has been approved by the Central Executive Committee of Turkestan. This involves the creation of an Uzbeg Republic (Uzbekistan) to include the Uzbegs inhabiting the present Turkestan Republic of Bokhara, of which a Tajik autonomous province will form part; also of a Turcoman Republic (Turkministan) to include the Turcomans of the former Transcaspian province, of Bokhara and of Khorezm. The Cossack Kirghiz population, living principally in the Syr Daria province, will be formed as a part of the Russian Socialist Federal Soviet Republic.

All this, if carried out, will sound the knell of departing mediaeval pomp, splendour, and picturesqueness, of which in its pre-war setting I have tried to give some faint idea. If in these pages my readers gain a little insight into the life of a people I have done my best to portray, a life that one can hardly even realize in this Western civilization of ours, the writer will feel herself amply repaid.